ROYAL COURT

The Royal Court Theatre & Liverpool Everyman and Playhouse present

ON TOUR
by **Gregory Burke**

First performance at The Royal Court Jerwood Theatre Upstairs
Sloane Square, London on 7 October 2005.

First performance at the Liverpool Everyman, Hope Street,
Liverpool on 28 October 2005.

Supported by Jerwood New Playwrights

JERWOOD
NEW PLAYWRIGHTS

This play was first developed at the National Theatre Studio

JERWOOD
NEW PLAYWRIGHTS

Since 1994 Jerwood New Playwrights has contributed to 47 new plays at the Royal Court including Joe Penhall's SOME VOICES, Mark Ravenhill's SHOPPING AND FUCKING (co-production with Out of Joint), Ayub Khan Din's EAST IS EAST (co-production with Tamasha), Martin McDonagh's THE BEAUTY QUEEN OF LEENANE (co-production with Druid Theatre Company), Conor McPherson's THE WEIR, Nick Grosso's REAL CLASSY AFFAIR, Sarah Kane's 4.48 PSYCHOSIS, Gary Mitchell's THE FORCE OF CHANGE, David Eldridge's UNDER THE BLUE SKY, David Harrower's PRESENCE, Simon Stephens' HERONS, Roy Williams' CLUBLAND, Leo Butler's REDUNDANT, Michael Wynne's THE PEOPLE ARE FRIENDLY, David Greig's OUTLYING ISLANDS, Zinnie Harris' NIGHTINGALE AND CHASE, Grae Cleugh's FUCKING GAMES, Rona Munro's IRON, Richard Bean's UNDER THE WHALEBACK, Ché Walker's FLESH WOUND, Roy Williams' FALLOUT, Mick Mahoney's FOOD CHAIN, Ayub Khan Din's NOTES ON FALLING LEAVES, Leo Butler's LUCKY DOG, Simon Stephens' COUNTRY MUSIC, Laura Wade's BREATHING CORPSES, Debbie Tucker Green's STONING MARY, David Eldridge's INCOMPLETE AND RANDOM ACTS OF KINDNESS.

This season Jerwood New Playwrights are supporting ON TOUR by Gregory Burke.

The Jerwood Charity is a registered charity dedicated to imaginative and responsible funding of the arts and other areas of human endeavour and excellence.

Leo Butler's LUCKY DOG
(photo: Ivan Kyncl)

David Eldridge's INCOMPLETE AND RANDOM
ACTS OF KINDNESS
(photo: Keith Pattison)

ON TOUR

by **Gregory Burke**

Cast (in order of appearance)
Daz **Paul Anderson**
H **Jeff Hordley**
Ray **Andrew Schofield**

Director **Matt Wilde**
Designer **Lisa Lillywhite**
Lighting Designer **Paul Anderson**
Sound Designer **Neil Alexander**
Composer **Jason Farrall**
Casting **Lisa Makin**
Production Manager **Sue Bird**
Stage Managers **Rebecca Austin, Hannah Ashwell-Dickinson**
Costume Supervisor **Iona Kenrick, Jackie Orton**
Company Voice Work **Patsy Rodenburg**
Fight Director **Terry King**

The Royal Court would like to thank the following for their help with this production:
Nicholas Gleaves, Burn Gorman, Lloyd Hutchinson, Daniel Mays, Nicholas Sidi,
Alan Stocks for all their work during the development of ON TOUR, Lucy Davies,
Natasha Bucknor and the staff of the National Theatre Studio.

THE COMPANY

Gregory Burke (writer)
Theatre includes: The Straits (Paines Plough/The Drum); Gagarin Way (Traverse/RNT/ West End); The Party (Headspace).
Radio includes: Occy Eyes.
Awards include: Critics' Circle Most Promising Playwright 2002, Best New Play at Barclays TMA Awards 2002 and Meyer-Whitworth Award 2002 for Gagarin Way; Pearson Best New Play Award 2003 for The Straits.

Neil Alexander (sound)
For the Royal Court: The Lying Kind, Yard Gal, Been So Long, Fair Game, Bailegangaire, Heredity and Penetrator.
Other theatre includes: The Laramie Project, Frankie and Johnny (Sound Theatre); Vanishing Points (Complicite); The Lemon Princess (West Yorkshire Playhouse); The Night Season, Democracy, Power, Elmina's Kitchen, Honour, She Stoops to Conquer/A Laughing Matter (with Out of Joint), A Prayer for Owen Meany, Life after Life, Vincent in Brixton, Mother Clap's Molly House, Marriage Play/Finding the Sun, Remembrance of Things Past, The Waiting Room, Blue Orange, Sparkleshark (RNT); The Little Fir Tree, Macbeth (Sheffield Crucible); The Arab-Israeli Cookbook, Two Horsemen (Gate); The Slab Boys, Cutting a Rug, Still Life (Traverse); Observe the Sons of Ulster Marching Towards the Somme, Normal - The Dusseldorf Ripper (Pleasance); The Snake House (Greenwich Studio); The Year of the Family (Finborough); Biloxi Blues (New Vanburgh).
Other design includes: Private Dancer (Brighton Art College).

Paul Anderson
Theatre includes: The Time of Your Life, The Long and the Short and the Tall, Three Sisters, Crimes of the Heart, The Lights, Brighton Beach Memoirs, The Mill on the Floss (Webber Douglas).
Paul Anderson has just graduated from Webber Douglas. This is his professional debut.
Television: Dr Who.

Paul Anderson (lighting designer)
For the Royal Court: Incomplete and Random Acts of Kindness.
Other theatre includes: Simply Heavenly, Arabian Nights, As I Lay Dying, Twelfth Night, Guys and Dolls, West Side Story (Young Vic); Someone Who'll Watch Over Me (West End); Turn of the Screw (Bristol Old Vic); Simply Heavenly (West End); A Minute Too Late, Stuff Happens, A Funny Thing Happened on the Way to the Forum, Measure for Measure, Cyrano de Bergerac, The Birds (RNT); The Resistible Rise of Arturo Ui (National Actors Theatre, New York); Lenny Henry's So Much Things to Say (West End/international tour); A Servant to Two Masters (RSC/West End); Twelfth Night (Middle Temple Hall); Singer, Americans, The Inland Sea (Oxford Stage Company); Taming of the Shrew (Salisbury Playhouse); 20,000 Leagues Under the Sea, Shoot to Win, Sleeping Beauty, Red Riding Hood, Aladdin, Cinderella (Theatre Royal, Stratford East); Strange Poetry (with the LA Philharmonic); The Elephant Vanishes, Light, The Noise of Time, Mnemonic (Drama Desk and Lucille Lortell awards); The Chairs (Theatre de Complicite); Some Girls are Bigger than Others, Pinocchio, The Threesome, Lyric Nights (Lyric Hammersmith); The Christie Brown Exhibition (Wapping Hydraulic Power Station); Rediscovering Pompeii (at the Accademia Italiana IBM Exhibition).
Paul has worked as lighting designer on fashion shows for Fashion East, Lancome, ghd and AI international.

Jason Farrall (composer)
Commercial releases include: Aquarel, Pura EP (1992 Network Records); Calvin Chambers Part 1 (1994 Sleeping Lion Records); Calvin Chambers Part 2 (1995 Sleeping Lion Records); Rhythm Saints Continuum (1996 N-Soul/Velocity Music Group); The Lithium Project, The Lithium Project (1997 Clear Recordings); The Lithium Project, Passo Fundo (2001 Hydrogen Dukebox Records); The Lithium Project, Many Worlds Theory (2003 Hydrogen Dukebox Records).
Remix Work includes: Inner City, Share my life (Aquarel, 6 x 6/Network Records UK); Slo Moshun, Help my friend (Aquarel, 6 x 6/Network Records UK); Rhythm Saints Continuum album (1996 N-Soul/Velocity Music Group); Reflection, The Morerroronus World, Another Sun (1997 Lithium Project, Clear Recordings).
TV Syncs include: Tony Hawks Gigantic Skate Park (2002 ESPN2 Background music for featured skaters); Derren Brown plays Russian Roulette (2003 Channel 4 UK).

Jeff Hordley

Theatre includes: Hidden Markings (Library Theatre/Homegrown Theatre); Miss Julie, Little Malcolm and His Struggle Against the Eunuchs (Bolton Octagon); An Acceptable Loss (Bolton Octagon); Young Playwrights (Manchester Contact); Peter Pan (Newbury Watermill).

Television includes: Emmerdale, City Central, Always and Everyone, The Ward, Coronation Street, Heartbeat.

Radio includes: The Taming of the Shrew, The Big Hot Summer, Atia (True Story), Close Enough to Touch, Pino Pelosi and the Boys, The Drover's Path, Lila, Silt, Bottle Blonde and Beautiful, An Inspector Calls, Violet's Dream.

Lisa Lillywhite (designer)

Theatre includes: Slowtime (RNT tour); Gong Donkeys, Got to be Happy, A Carpet, A Pony and a Monkey, Blackbird (Bush); Lady Windermere's Fan (Pegasus Theatre, Oxford); The Lisbon Traviata (King's Head); Tape (Soho); Live from Golgotha, PWA - The Diaries of Oscar Moore (Drill Hall); Modern Love (RFH); The Changeling (Southwark); Passion (Chelsea); Young Hamlet (Young Vic); The Club (Old Red Lion); Musical Youth (Birmingham Rep); Dutchman (Etcetera); Dwarfs/The Local Stigmatic (Lyric Studio); Prometheus In Evin, Brighton Beach Scumbags (Brockley Jack); A Midsummer Night's Dream (Newark Theatre).

Design for Television includes: Princes Trust Urban Music Festival, Smash Hits Poll Winners Party 2004.

Awards: Arts Foundation Stage Design Fellowship Award 2001.

Andrew Schofield

Theatre includes: Of Mice and Men (Old Vic); Breezeblock Park, Scouse, Dr Faustus, No Holds Barred (Liverpool Everyman); Neville's Island, A Christmas Carol, Sgt. Peppers Magical Mystery Trip, Be Bop A Lula, One for the Road, Cavern of Dreams, Stags and Hens, Erpingham Camp, April First Show, Blood on the Dole (Liverpool Playhouse); Seven Ages of Woman (Liverpool Playhouse/tour); Self Catering, 8 Miles High, Two (Liverpool Playhouse Studio).

Musicals include: Blood Brothers (Lyric Theatre); John, Paul, George, Ringo and Bert (Nottingham Playhouse); Sweeney Todd (Half Moon); Cinderella and her Rockin' Fella (Liverpool Everyman).

Television includes: Murphy's Law, Donovan, Holby City, Nice Guy Eddie, Stan the Man, City Central, Maisie Raine, Oliver Twist, Casualty, Melissa, Thieftakers, Jake's Progress, Rules of Engagement, The Bill, Blood on the Dole, Doomsday Gun, Self Catering, Requiem Apache, The Long Road, Boon, Scully, G.B.H., Stay Lucky, Needle, El Cid, The Marksman, Kidnapped, Death of a Young Young Man, Z Cars, Coronation Street, Boys from the Black Stuff.

Film includes: Under The Mud, Revengers Tragedy, Heap of Trouble, Liam, There's Only One Jimmy Grimble, Sharkhunt, Hamlet, Sid and Nancy, No Surrender, Distant Voices Still Lives, Dead Mavis Cards.

Matt Wilde (director)

Matt Wilde is a former Associate Director at the National Theatre Studio and has worked extensively as a Staff and Associate Director for the National Theatre and Out of Joint.

Theatre includes: Slow Time by Roy Williams (RNT Education tour), His Dark Materials as revival co-director (RNT Olivier), Portugal (rehearsed reading, RNT Cottesloe), Criminals (RNT Studio): The Insatiate Countess (Young Vic Studio); Romeo and Juliet, Macbeth (Southwark Playhouse).

THE ENGLISH STAGE COMPANY
AT THE ROYAL COURT

The English Stage Company at the Royal Court opened in 1956 as a subsidised theatre producing new British plays, international plays and some classical revivals.

The first artistic director George Devine aimed to create a writers' theatre, 'a place where the dramatist is acknowledged as the fundamental creative force in the theatre and where the play is more important than the actors, the director, the designer'. The urgent need was to find a contemporary style in which the play, the acting, direction and design are all combined. He believed that 'the battle will be a long one to continue to create the right conditions for writers to work in'.

Devine aimed to discover 'hard-hitting, uncompromising writers whose plays are stimulating, provocative and exciting'. The Royal Court production of John Osborne's Look Back in Anger in May 1956 is now seen as the decisive starting point of modern British drama and the policy created a new generation of British playwrights. The first wave included John Osborne, Arnold Wesker, John Arden, Ann Jellicoe, N F Simpson and Edward Bond. Early seasons included new international plays by Bertolt Brecht, Eugène Ionesco, Samuel Beckett, Jean-Paul Sartre and Marguerite Duras.

The theatre started with the 400-seat proscenium arch Theatre Downstairs, and in 1969 opened a second theatre, the 60-seat studio Theatre Upstairs. Some productions transfer to the West End, such as Terry Johnson's Hitchcock Blonde, Caryl Churchill's Far Away and Conor McPherson's The Weir. Recent touring productions include Sarah Kane's 4.48 Psychosis (US tour) and Ché Walker's Flesh Wound (Galway Arts Festival). The Royal Court also co-produces plays which transfer to the West End or tour internationally, such as Conor McPherson's Shining City (with Gate Theatre, Dublin), Sebastian Barry's The Steward of Christendom and Mark Ravenhill's Shopping and Fucking (with Out of Joint), Martin McDonagh's The Beauty Queen Of Leenane (with Druid), Ayub Khan Din's East is East (with Tamasha).

Since 1994 the Royal Court's artistic policy has again been vigorously directed to finding and producing a new generation of playwrights. The writers include Joe Penhall, Rebecca Prichard, Michael Wynne, Nick Grosso, Judy Upton, Meredith Oakes, Sarah Kane, Anthony Neilson, Judith Johnson, James Stock, Jez Butterworth, Marina Carr, Phyllis Nagy, Simon Block, Martin

photo: Andy Chopping

McDonagh, Mark Ravenhill, Ayub Khan Din, Tamantha Hammerschlag, Jess Walters, Ché Walker, Conor McPherson, Simon Stephens, Richard Bean, Roy Williams, Gary Mitchell, Mick Mahoney, Rebecca Gilman, Christopher Shinn, Kia Corthron, David Gieselmann, Marius von Mayenburg, David Eldridge, Leo Butler, Zinnie Harris, Grae Cleugh, Roland Schimmelpfennig, Chloe Moss, DeObia Oparei, Enda Walsh, Vassily Sigarev, the Presnyakov Brothers, Marcos Barbosa, Lucy Prebble, John Donnelly, Clare Pollard, Robin French, Elyzabeth Gregory Wilder, Rob Evans, Laura Wade and Debbie Tucker Green. This expanded programme of new plays has been made possible through the support of A.S.K. Theater Projects and the Skirball Foundation, The Jerwood Charity, the American Friends of the Royal Court Theatre and (in 1994/5 and 1999) in association with the National Theatre Studio.

In recent years there have been record-breaking productions at the box office, with capacity houses for Joe Penhall's Dumb Show, Conor McPherson's Shining City, Roy Williams' Fallout and Terry Johnson's Hitchcock Blonde.

The refurbished theatre in Sloane Square opened in February 2000, with a policy still inspired by the first artistic director George Devine. The Royal Court is an international theatre for new plays and new playwrights, and the work shapes contemporary drama in Britain and overseas.

PROGRAMME SUPPORTERS

The Royal Court (English Stage Company Ltd) receives its principal funding from Arts Council England, London. It is also supported financially by a wide range of private companies, charitable and public bodies, and earns the remainder of its income from the box office and its own trading activities.

The Genesis Foundation supports International Playwrights and the Young Writers' Festival. The Jerwood Charity supports new plays by new playwrights through the Jerwood New Playwrights series.

The Skirball Foundation funds a Playwrights' Programme at the theatre. The Artistic Director's Chair is supported by a lead grant from The Peter Jay Sharp Foundation, contributing to the activities of the Artistic Director's office. Bloomberg Mondays, the Royal Court's reduced price ticket scheme, is supported by Bloomberg. Over the past eight years the BBC has supported the Gerald Chapman Fund for directors.

ROYAL COURT
SLOANE SQUARE

11–29 October
Jerwood Theatre Downstairs

MY NAME IS RACHEL CORRIE

Taken from the writings of
Rachel Corrie
Edited by **Alan Rickman** and
Katharine Viner

director **Alan Rickman**
design **Hildegard Bechtler**
lighting design **Johanna Town**
sound and video design **Emma Laxton**

cast **Megan Dodds**

MY NAME IS RACHEL CORRIE has been developed in collaboration with the Royal Court International Department with the kind permission of Rachel Corrie's family

28 October –26 November
Jerwood Theatre Upstairs

THE WORLD'S BIGGEST DIAMOND
by **Gregory Motton**

A cottage by the sea. Two old lovers re-unite for a weekend after 30 years. He has an appointment with death, and she has left her husband upstairs. Both think the other has betrayed their love. They fight it out as a storm grows out at sea.

director **Simon Usher**
design **Anthony Lamble**

cast: **Jane Asher, Michael Feast**

BOX OFFICE
020 7565 5000
BOOK ONLINE
www.royalcourttheatre.com

ARTS COUNCIL ENGLAND

LIVERPOOL EVERYMAN AND PLAYHOUSE

About the Theatres

In 2000, two great regional reps were merged into a single company. At the beginning of 2004, buoyed up by Liverpool's impending status as European Capital of Culture in 2008, they entered a new and dynamic era. By returning to producing on a major scale, the Everyman and Playhouse have reclaimed their place on the national stage and generated an energy that has attracted acclaim, awards and audience loyalty.

The Liverpool Everyman and Playhouse theatres are always looking to bring the people of Merseyside a rich and varied portrait of the theatrical landscape. We have a strong and passionate commitment to new writing. Today's playwrights are tomorrow's theatrical legacy.

While this play has a particular resonance for a Liverpool audience there can be no doubt that it is a play that illuminates our national cultural position. It is with great pleasure that we present *On Tour* by Gregory Burke in partnership with The Royal Court Theatre London whose reputation for the nurturing and production of new writing is second to none.

Liverpool Everyman and Playhouse would like to thank all our current supporters:

Corporate Members Benson Signs; Bibby Factors Northwest Ltd; Brabners Chaffe Street; C3 Imaging; Chadwick Chartered Accountants; Dawsons Music Ltd; Duncan Sheard Glass; DWF Solicitors; Grant Thornton; Hope Street Hotel; HSBC Bank Plc; John Lewis; Mando Group; Nonconform Design; Nviron Ltd; Oddbins; Synergy Colour Printing; The Famous Bankrupt Shop; The Workbank; Victor Huglin Carpets.

Trusts & Grant-Making Bodies BBC Northern Exposure; BBC Radio Merseyside; The Eleanor Rathbone Charitable Trust; Five; The Granada Foundation; Henry Cotton Memorial Fund; Liverpool Culture Company; P H Holt Charitable Trust.

This theatre has the support of the Pearson's Playwrights' Scheme sponsored by Pearson plc. Assisted by the Co-operative Group through Business in the Arts: North West.

Individual Supporters Peter and Geraldine Bounds, George C Carver, Councillor Eddie Clein, Mr & Mrs Dan Hugo, A. Thomas Jackson, Ms D. Leach, Frank D Paterson, Les Read, Sheena Streather, Frank D Thompson, DB Williams and all those who prefer to remain anonymous.

Liverpool Everyman and Playhouse is a registered charity no, 1081229
www.everymanplayhouse.com

Funders

The City of Liverpool

KNOWSLEY
METROPOLITAN BOROUGH

Sefton Council

Metropolitan
Borough of Wirral

NEW WRITING AT LIVERPOOL EVERYMAN AND PLAYHOUSE

"A remarkable renaissance"
(Liverpool Daily Post)

As Liverpool prepares to take on the mantle of European Capital of Culture in 2008, the Everyman and Playhouse have entered an extremely dynamic period. The theatres' revival began in 2004, driven by a major expansion in production and by a passionate commitment to new writing.

On Tour is the latest in a rich and varied slate of world, european or regional premières which has been enthusiastically received by Merseyside audiences and helped to put Liverpool's theatre back on the national map.

"Lyrical, muscular, full of indignation and compassion"
(The Sunday Times on Yellowman)

Highly acclaimed productions have included the European première of Yellowman by Dael Orlandsmith, which transferred to Hampstead Theatre and will tour nationally in spring 2006, and regional premières of Conor McPherson's Port Authority and Simon Block's Chimps. And in just eighteen months, the theatres have produced four world premières of plays developed and nurtured in Liverpool - Fly by Katie Douglas; The Kindness of Strangers by Tony Green; Urban Legend by Laurence Wilson, and most recently The Morris by Helen Blakeman.

"The Everyman could wish for no finer 40th anniversary present than a return to form"
(The Guardian on The Kindness of Strangers)

Around the main production programme, the theatres run a range of projects and activities to create opportunities and offer support to writers at every career stage. The commissioning programme invests in the creation of new work for both the Everyman and the Playhouse stages. The Henry Cotton Writers on Attachment scheme is providing three young Liverpool writers with an intensive programme of creative and career development. Thanks to Five and to Pearson TV both Laurence Wilson and Tony Green will benefit from year-long residencies. And an annual new writing festival, Everyword, offers a busy and popular week of seminars, sofa talks and work-in-progress readings.

"Laurence Wilson is another name to add to the theatre's long and glorious reputation for nurturing new talent"
(Liverpool Echo on Urban Legend)

The full programme at the Everyman and Playhouse blends this new work with bold interpretations of classic drama, and mixes our own Made in Liverpool productions with carefully hand-picked touring shows. By doing so, we aim to offer the people of Merseyside a rich and satisfying theatrical diet. But if we are driven by one thing more than all others, it is the conviction that an investment in new writing is an investment in our theatrical future.

For more information about the Everyman and Playhouse – including the full programme, off-stage activities such as playwright support, and ways in which you can support our investment in talent – visit www.everymanplayhouse.com.

Gregory Burke
On Tour

ff
faber and faber

First published in 2005
by Faber and Faber Limited
3 Queen Square London WC1N 3AU

Typeset by Country Setting, Kingsdown, Kent CT14 8ES
Printed in England by Mackays of Chatham plc, Chatham, Kent

A CIP record for this book
is available from the British Library

ISBN 0–571–23171–3

2 4 6 8 10 9 7 5 3 1

To Brian and Elizabeth Burke

Acknowledgements

The author would like to thank

The National Theatre Studio
for their help and support in the development
of this play.

Lucy Davies and all her staff for their input,
encouragement and cups of tea.

Natasha Bucknor.

All the actors who workshopped the play:
Burn Gorman, Nicholas Sidi, Alan Stocks,
Nicholas Gleaves, Lloyd Hutchinson, Daniel Mays.

Jack Bradley for putting myself and Matt Wilde
together after we both had very hazy ideas about
being interested in, or perhaps thinking about, maybe
doing something that might have something
to do with football culture.

Gemma Bodinetz and Deborah Aydon and all at the
Liverpool Everyman.

Ian Rickson and everybody at the Royal Court.

Alan Brodie and Lisa Foster and everybody at ABR.

And, of course, Matt Wilde.

Thank you.

Characters

Daz
a cockney

H
a manc

Ray
a scouser

Act One

A cell in a police station. The cell has a bed against opposite walls. The door in the far wall has a spyhole. Two men share the cell. Daz, in his mid-twenties, is sitting on the bed on one side of the cell. H, in his mid-thirties, sits on the opposite bed. Daz is examining two banknotes. Both are dressed 'football casual'-style.

H (*leans forward, smiling*) I knew you wouldn't be able to get it.

Daz Give us a chance.

H You been at it ten fuckin minutes.

Daz turns the notes over slowly. He lifts one up so that he can look at it against a light.

Daz Fuckin light in here's terrible.

Daz stands up and moves directly under the light.

H Sure you don't need glasses?

Daz squints at it, rubs his eyes and squints at it again. He lifts the note up to the light beside the first one. He squints from one to the other.

Come on. Come on.

Daz has one last look.

Daz I ain't got a clue, mate.

H Guess.

Daz I dunno.

H Fuckin guess.

Daz (*loud*) I don't fuckin know.

H Have a fuckin guess.

   Pause.

Daz (*holding out one of the notes*) This one.

H This one's the fake or this one's the real one?

Daz It's this one.

H This one's the fake or this one's the real?

Daz Yeah.

   Pause.

What?

H You said this one's what?

Daz I said this is the one.

H Which one?

Daz This one.

H Yeah, but which one did you say this one was? The fake or the real?

   Pause.

Daz That's the fake.

   Pause.

H (*smiles*) That's the fuckin real.

Daz Bollocks.

H It is.

Daz (*looks again*) You sure?

H I knew you wouldn't get it.

Daz (*takes the note back. He looks at it*) They look good.

H Yeah.

Daz Detailed.

H It's the beard.

Pause.

Daz (*turning the note over*) Who is he?

H Who the fuck is he?

Daz Yeah.

H Charles Darwin?

Pause.

On the Origin of the Species by Means of Natural Selection; or the Preservation of Favoured Races in the Struggle for Life?

Pause.

The Descent of Man?

Daz shrugs. H. shakes his head.

Fuckin hell. (*Takes the note back and studies it.*) All your money. It's always the same. (*Beat.*) Writer. Composer. Prime Minister. King. (*Beat.*) Someone vitally important to the national sense of self. (*Beat.*) Preferably with a 'tache.

Daz With a 'tache?

H Or a beard. (*Beat.*) Even an unruly hairstyle does the job. (*Beat.*) Hair is very important to your treasuries. Difficult to forge, hair. (*Beat.*) The detail. (*Beat.*) That's why Einstein's very popular at your mints. (*Beat.*) Universally known. Moustache. Mad hair. Got the fuckin lot.

Pause.

Art Garfunkel.

Daz You what?

H Art. Garfunkel. (*Beat.*) I reckon he'll be popular. In currency, in the future. (*Beat.*) Course your counterfeitin community would prefer Kojak. (*Kisses the note.*) Who loves ya, baby? (*Holds the note up to the light.*) Cotton fibre, linen-rag mix. Images of the *Beagle* an a Galapagos Island hummingbird. Holographic foil patch with an image of Britannia just beneath the serial number on the left-hand side. (*Beat.*) Windowed metallic thread an a watermark of Her Majesty that actually looks like her. (*Beat.*) This is fuckin good work. (*He pulls another note from his pocket and gives it to Daz.*) Your twenty is Elgar.

Daz Is it?

H 'Pomp and Circumstance'? (*Beat.*) 'Land of Hope and Glory'?

Daz I'm more a 'Rule Britannia' man myself.

H Rule Britannia.

Pause.

Britannia rules the waves.

Pause.

Britons never, never, never.

Pause.

Shall be slaves.

Pause.

You ever been a slave?

Daz No.

H Me neither. (*Puts out his hand.*) Pleased to meet you.

  Daz looks at H's hand. Then shakes.

H H.

Daz H?

H Yeah.

Daz What does that stand for?

H (*shrugs*) Everyone calls me H.

  Pause.

Daz Daz.

H Daz?

Daz Everyone calls me Daz.

  Pause.

H First time in Scandinavia, Daz?

Daz Yeah. (*Hands the note back to H.*)

H You keep that, mate.

Daz Cheers.

  Pause.

You know a lot about money, then?

H I fuckin love the stuff. (*Beat.*) Don't you like money?

Daz I ain't bothered.

H You ain't bothered?

  Pause.

You ain't a fuckin socialist are you?

Daz Do I look like a socialist?

H It's so fuckin difficult to tell these days.

Daz I just mean, you know, as long as I've got clothes and stuff and some on me hip. (*Beat.*) I've never wanted to be rich or nothin.

H No?

Daz No.

    Pause.

H The best fuckin thing in the world, mate. Money.

    Pause.

I can let you have some of this stuff when we get out?

Daz You're alright.

H Half face-value.

Daz I'm fine.

H Sure?

Daz I'll think about it.

H You'll think about it?

Daz Yeah.

    Pause.

H Anythin else you want?

Daz I wouldn't mind gettin out of here.

H Sunglasses?

Daz No.

H Gucci. Very nice.

Daz No.

H How about a watch?

Daz (*pulls up his sleeve*) I've got a watch.

H (*looks at it*) No. These are good watches. Tag Heuer. Rolex.

Daz Fakes?

H Hundred per cent genuine. In the box. Manufacturer's certificate of authenticity. (*Beat.*) Electronic stuff? (*Beat.*) I can get hold of those great little iPods. The colour ones. (*Beat.*) Chipped phone? (*Beat.*) Viagra? (*Beat.*) Credit cards? (*Beat.*) CS gas? (*Beat.*) Stun-guns?

Daz Guns?

H Stun-guns. Little ones. Tiny. Put it in the palm of your hand, sneak up on someone. Zap. They're on their arse.

Daz Firearms?

Pause.

H Take a couple of phone calls.

Daz What can you get?

H Depends how much you've got to spend.

Pause.

I don't really like gettin guns. You gotta mix with the wrong sort of people. You know what I mean?

Pause.

You goin to Germany in the summer?

Daz Course. Yeah.

H (*holds up the notes*) That's the time to pass these, mate. When the place is awash with muppets in replica shirts. Sunburnt and drunk. Every bar's packed, staff are rushed off their feet. No one's payin a blind bit of notice. Piece of piss.

Daz (*gets up and looks through the spyhole in the door, turns back to face the room*) What d'you reckon they'll do with us?

H Dunno.

Daz D'you reckon we'll get deported?

H If they were gonna deport us we'd be on our way to the airport by now.

Pause.

The copper that booked me in said they'd let us go after the match. (*Looks at his watch*) What d'you reckon? An hour.

Pause.

Daz I dunno why they fuckin nicked us in the first place.

H You know what it's like. A football match, someone drops their pint glass. They arrest every Anglo-Saxon in a ten-mile radius. (*Beat.*) How else do they justify all the riot police?

Daz Where d'you get nicked?

H The station. I was just comin out of left-luggage when a trainload arrived. Obviously the sight of so many English people in a train terminus was too much for them an they decided to throw their weight around.

Daz They got me there an all.

H You on the train?

Daz In the station. Left-luggage. I'd just stuck my bag in and bang. I wasn't doin nothin.

H Everyone's always doin nothin.

Daz I was mindin me own business. Fuckers.

H Mate of mine got deported from Italy. Rimini, 1990, durin the World Cup. On the plane next to him was this American bloke who was on his honeymoon. This Yank, he'd only nipped out to get a packet of fags an an *International Herald Tribune*. There's a fight in a bar down the road an the next thing he knows he's at fuckin Gatwick. No passport, nothin.

Daz I bet his missus didn't believe him neither.

H My mate had to take him into London to their embassy. (*Beat.*) Still gets a Christmas card from the cunt.

   Pause.

I were a bit surprised today. I thought they weren't like that here. I thought they respected your civil rights in this part of the world. (*Beat.*) Riot police. Law unto themselves, ain't they.

Daz Yeah. (*Beat.*) They were alright in here, though.

H Very polite.

Daz They didn't even fuckin search me properly.

H Me neither.

Daz They had a quick look through my wallet then gave it back.

H I thought one of them was gonna have me watch off me, but I think he were wondering whether it were nicked or not.

Daz Is it?

H Not from here. Prague. Before the Germany game. We stopped off on the way to Munich. Got it off some young lads who did a jeweller's.

   Pause.

No, they won't tax you here. They're very law-abidin people. (*Beat.*) Even the coppers.

Pause.

Shit comin all this way an missin the match.

Daz Fuck the match.

H Is that not what you're here for?

Daz Well, yeah . . . but you know. Fuck it. (*Beat.*) Now.

Pause.

Didn't have a ticket anyway.

H I could have sorted you out a ticket.

Daz Yeah?

H Not in our end. You'd be in with the locals.

Daz I ain't bothered. It ain't about havin a ticket is it? It's about the craic.

Pause.

H That's a funny thing that innit?

Daz What is?

H The amount of time English fans spend in Irish bars when they're abroad.

Daz They're everywhere, though, ain't they? (*Beat.*) An you get a decent pint.

H It's a bit strange though innit, when you're sittin with everyone singin 'No Surrender to the IRA' in a pub called O'fuckin Reilly's . . .

Pause.

You ever think about that?

Pause.

Daz You been to Ireland, then?

H Yeah.

Daz Belfast?

H I haven't, as it happens. (*Beat.*) But I hear it's very nice.

The spyhole in the cell door goes back and someone looks in. It snaps shut again. H gets up and listens at the cell door. He comes back to the bunks and puts his hand down the front of his trousers and fiddles about. He pulls out a wrap.

I suppose I better get rid of this. Just in case they do decide to search us proper.

H smells the wrap.

Daz You ain't had it up your arse, have you?

H No. Just tucked . . . tucked up under me sack.

He removes the cling film and throws it into the corner of the cell. He opens the bag and pours some of the powder on to the back of his hand. He offers the bag to Daz.

Daz I'm alright, mate.

H It's not been up me arse. Honest.

Daz You sure?

H Course I'm fuckin sure. (*Beat.*) I know when somethin's been up me arse.

Daz takes the bag and sniffs it.

It ain't been up me arse.

Daz When did you last have a wash?

H If you don't want any it's fine.

Daz No. (*Pours some cocaine from the bag onto the back of his hand.*) I want some.

H (*pulls out one of his notes*) Use the fake. Cover it in charlie, it'll feel even more real.

He rolls up the fake note and snorts some cocaine off the back of his hand. Daz hesitates, looking at the door, then takes a line. H has already chopped out more on his hand. He takes this. Daz takes another line.

Daz (*unrolls the fake note and looks at it*) So where d'you get these, then?

H I've got this mate. This Danish bloke. I went to see him on the way here.

Daz How d'you know him?

H I did a bit of time over there.

Daz Yeah?

H (*nods*) Just out.

Pause.

Daz What was that for?

H Oh, it were fuck-all really. But I met this bloke. We got on sound. I did a couple of things for him an he said give us a call when you get out.

Daz An he's a counterfeiter?

H He does a bit of everythin. You know, he's got a couple of bars an stuff. A few flats. He does all sorts, motors, gear. Jack of all trades. Even has a few girls working for him. (*Beat.*) In fact, if you're ever in Copenhagen an you need a girl, some gear an a brand new motor, he's your man.

Pause.

But it's all just a front for the gear.

Daz Proper gangster is he?

H I think he prefers businessman.

Daz Don't they all?

H He's a sort of a biker.

Daz A biker?

H There's other gangs, you know, Russians an Turks an Albanians, the same as everywhere else. But the locals are all in these biker gangs. They don't look like bikers. It's all short hair and suits and stuff, but they're bikers when they start out, that's how they get known, but they get a bit more subtle when they get older. They're into everythin. An you gotta take them serious when they can do – (*Holds up the note.*) stuff of this quality.

Pause.

An they're fuckin mental.

Daz What are they, Hell's Angels?

H No. What is it? Bandidos.

Daz Arse Bandidos.

H (*laughs*) You wouldn't be saying that if you met these cunts. Fuckin loonys, they are. I went to one of their clubhouses, this bar, and you want to see the stuff they were showing me, machine guns, rocket launchers, grenades, the fuckin lot. When they have a war, it's a proper war.

Daz Bollocks.

H What? (*Beat.*) You don't think they can have a war?

Daz I just find it fuckin funny when people say let's have a fuckin war, they dunno what the fuck they're talkin about.

H These boys know what they're talkin about.

Daz It depends what sort of fuckin war you're talking about.

H A war's a fuckin war, ain't it?

Daz People shouldn't use that word when they dunno what the fuck it means.

Pause.

I was in the Royal Marines.

Pause.

H I bet you're glad you're not still in. You'd be over in fuckin Basra.

Daz My old unit haven't had to go yet.

H No?

Daz Not yet.

H Lucky them, I mean, who the fuck'd fancy fuckin that. Sitting, fuckin shittin yourself, waiting for some fuckin suicide bombers to drive up to you every day.

Pause.

It's fucked-up, innit?

Daz Well, that's because the fuckin Yanks are involved. Fuckin cowboys, ain't they? All they're good for is nickin kit off. (*Beat.*) They call us the borrowers, you know, cause the British nick so much kit off them. (*Beat.*) Some blokes I know who were in Saudi before the war said they had these warehouses in their bases full of stuff. Sent over from America for their soldiers. Stereos. Tellys.

PlayStations. All sent to keep their morale up. The British units were drivin up in trucks an just loadin up. Blokes were sendin stuff home for their kids goin, 'That's next Christmas taken care of.'

H I knew a bloke who was in Iraq in the first Gulf War.

Daz My lot, 45 Commando, they were in the north when all the Kurds got fucked over. You know, when they had the uprisin an that, but then Saddam got back in an they all got fuckin massacred.

H He said . . .

Daz Some of the older lads used to talk about that. It wasn't just the Iraqis they had to stop either, the Turkish were doin them as well. They always get fucked-over, the Kurds.

H Yeah . . .

Daz They've got a sayin. A Kurd has no friends.

H He . . .

Daz Bastards, the Turkish. I fuckin hate them.

H Ancient emnity, though. (*Beat.*) Wherever you get a Turk and a Kurd together. You get a row.

   Pause.

Should have left the Ottoman Empire alone. All your grief in your Middle East's down to the Ottoman Empire fuckin up. (*Beat.*) An your Balfour Declaration obviously.

Daz Yeah . . . obviously.

H (*takes the wrap back out*) Better finish this. (*He chops the last of the cocaine out and throws the wrap under one of the beds.*) Oh yeah. Root of the whole fuckin thing, the Balfour Declaration. (*He takes a line of cocaine.*) What was it?

Daz What?

H The thing about Palestine bein Palestine apart from some lands west of the Jordan which ain't exclusively Arab. Or summat. (*Beat.*) If you're gonna be that fuckin vague you're askin for trouble, aren't you?

Daz Yeah.

H I were in prison in Turkey once.

Daz Yeah?

H Not for very long, thank fuck.

Daz Rough was it?

H It were a fuckin nightmare. (*Takes a line of cocaine.*) They don't have cells over there, either. (*Stands up.*) It was like a big dormitory. Dozens of cunts in there. I used to sleep with the fuckin sheets tied round my waist. (*Offers Daz some more cocaine.*)

Daz Shit.

H Yeah. That were the most dangerous time. When you went for a shit. It were just a fuckin hole dug in the yard. They used to wait an ambush you when it were halfway out your arse.

Daz (*takes a line*) Fuck off.

H It were terrifyin. But I were young. I didn't give a fuck, did I? (*Beat.*) I got friendly with a few political prisoners there. They had their own wing. Separate from the rest. They ain't daft, the Turks. They keep all the political prisoners together. They know not to put them in with the criminals. That's when you get the real problems. You put one political prisoner in a cell with ten hardened criminals, you don't end up with one less political prisoner. You end up with ten hardened revolutionaries. The political prisoners get people organised. If a government's got a clue it keeps them separate. Otherwise they end up in trouble.

Pause.

When d'you leave the army, then?

Daz About a year an a bit ago.

H What d'you come out for?

Daz (*shrugs*) I got a bit bored in the end. Runnin about fuckin Dartmoor all day with a hundred pounds of kit on me back.

H What are you up to now?

Daz I've been doin the doors an that. Security.

H Security? (*Beat.*) Haven't you got any ambition, mate?

Daz I've got an ambition to get out of here.

H Come on. You've got skills. You've got a market value. Familiar with weapons, tactics. (*Beat.*) Oldest profession in the world, mate, violence. You can make a lot of money if you know the right people. (*Beat.*) You must get a chance to earn a bit when you're in the forces, you know, in war zones an that.

Daz Well, it depends really. I mean some blokes are always on the lookout for a bit of pilfering. There was a lot of it went on in Kosovo.

H Ottoman Empire again. (*Beat.*) The reason there's Muslims in the Balkans.

Daz There were a lot of mercenaries around down there. All sorts goin on with the KLA. Drugs an kidnappin an stuff . . .

H You've never thought about doin anythin like that? Mercenary work?

Daz Fightin someone else's war don't interest me.

H Must be a lot of opportunities in it.

Daz Lot of opportunities to get killed.

H Yeah, but you look at war zones. (*Beat.*) Yeah they're dangerous when there's fightin, but once the fightin stops there's always money to be made. (*Beat.*) The trick is to get in there at just the right moment. It's like Russia, you know, Communism collapsed and there was chaos, but chaos is good from a business point of view. Chaos gives you a window of opportunity. That's how the Russian mafia took over. They were on their toes. They were ready for the opportunity. All these fuckin billionaires buyin up fuckin London an swannin about the fuckin Costa del Sol. How the fuck did they get their money? Fuckin raped their own country an fucked off before the government could get its act together. (*Beat.*) Good fuckin luck to them. (*Beat.*) Law. Regulation. Policing. It all takes that little bit of time to get its act together. It always lags a little bit behind. (*Beat.*) Anarchy is opportunity. (*Beat.*) Someone like you. Who knows what they're doin? (*Beat.*) Don't you wanna make a few quid?

Pause.

Daz I was thinkin about joinin the Foreign Legion.

H Fuckin hell.

Pause.

I had a mate did that.

Daz Yeah?

H He never made it.

Daz It's a tough unit.

H No. I mean he got shot by a farmer on his way down there to sign up.

Daz Dead?

H No. It was just like a coupla shotgun pellets in his arse. (*Beat.*) He were a right stupid fucker.

Pause.

Daz What you sayin?

H What?

Daz You think I'm fuckin stupid?

H No.

Daz You think people are in the forces cause they can't do nothin else?

H I didn't mean it like that.

Daz (*gets up*) It fuckin sounds like it. (*He starts to do press-ups.*)

H I know it ain't all bad, the forces. (*Lies back on his bunk watching him.*) They reckon it soaks up a certain percentage of the country's psychopaths for one thing.

Daz (*continuing with his press-ups*) Where you from, mate?

H Where do I live?

Daz Yeah.

Pause.

H I suppose, technically, I'm homeless.

Daz (*stops and gets up*) But where you from?

H England.

Daz Whereabouts?

H What does it matter?

Daz What team are you with?

H I'm just England, mate.

Daz You must have a club?

H No.

Daz What, never? Where you from? You're a manc, ain't you?

H Yeah.

Daz So what manc club then?

H United when I were a kid, but . . .

Daz What's a United fan following England for?

H . . . my heart went out of it when they went PLC.

Daz United all fuckin hate England. You should be followin Ireland.

H What about you?

Daz What about me?

H I'm guessin Chelsea.

Daz (*laughs*) I come over with some West Ham.

H You're an Iron?

Daz No.

H Mind your backs.

Daz I know a few of them.

H So . . . who are ya?

Pause.

Daz Well, you know, with bein in the Marines. I ain't lived back home for a while. (*Beat.*) And I lived in foster homes when I was a kid.

H Yeah?

Daz Yeah.

Pause.

H So you don't really come from nowhere?

Daz No. (*Beat.*) I don't suppose I do.

H Must be nice, that? (*Beat.*) Comin from nowhere? (*Beat.*) No ties. No attachments. (*Beat.*) Nothin in your life you can't walk out on in thirty seconds if you spot the heat round the corner. (*Beat.*) You're free. (*Beat.*) You're lucky. There's not many people get that luxury. (*Beat.*) It's very useful.

Daz You think?

H Yeah. (*Beat.*) Take today. (*Beat.*) What did you come here for?

Pause.

Daz Same as you.

H No you didn't.

Daz I did.

H No, mate, you did not come here for the same thing as me.

Daz So what did you come here for?

H I came here on business.

Daz Business?

H Yeah.

Daz Well, you look like a lad to me.

H Well, I am a lad.

Daz A bit old. (*Beat.*) But still a lad.

H See, I know why you're here today.

Daz To follow England.

H And?

Daz And . . .

H An have a row?

Daz (*shrugs*) Be rude not to.

H I used to do it myself. What else is there to do when you're young an full of beans? There'd be somethin wrong with you if you didn't like a fight.

Daz You're still doin it.

H No. I'm not. (*Beat.*) See, you have to move on, do different things. Evolve. (*Beat.*) Fighting's a young man's game. I don't care how hard you are, I'd take a pack of sixteen-year-olds against anyone.

Daz You reckon?

H All that testosterone. Fuckin hell.

Daz Suppose.

H But what that fightin does, what all these young lads provide, is opportunity. (*Beat.*) What d'you always get when we play abroad?

Daz Beat.

H Chaos. (*Beat.*) Guaranteed fuckin chaos. Like we were sayin. About war. (*Beat.*) Now I know this is nothin like war, but there's always the potential of a little bit of trouble. A little bit of anarchy. A little bit of chaos.

(*Beat.*) Some of us are here to take advantage of the chaos. (*Beat.*) You said you didn't have a ticket?

Daz Yeah.

H Did you try an get one?

Daz I didn't get a fuckin chance.

H But if you did? The touts are always English?

Daz Yeah.

H You go to buy some gear. Bit of showbiz sherbet to keep you out drinking for a couple of days? There's English blokes dealin in every pub. Pin-badges? English. Replica kits? English. Snide clobber? English. If it kicks off, which I doubt with this bein a friendly, then every sports shop in this city'll get hit. Jewellers' windows'll be goin in. Robberies. When? (*Beat.*) When all your local constabulary's runnin around chasin some fat bloke with tattoos who's thrown a plastic chair.

Daz (*shrugs*) That's what happens. That's England away.

H Not England. Grafters. Spivs. On the make. (*Beat.*) Briefs, fags, snides, smash 'n' grabs . . . gear . . . whatever it is. We're takin advantage. (*Beat.*) We might be goin to games. We might be followin England everywhere, all over the world. But what we're really followin is the opportunities that it provides.

   Pause.

A few years ago I'd have been out there, roamin around lookin for the locals. Tryin to prove a point. Tryin to live up to the image of the northern barbarians. (*Beat.*) I don't see the point in throwing a punch when you don't gain nothin from it. Not any more. Throw a punch if you're gonna earn. There ain't a country in the world that goes to war for anythin but gain, so why should you?

31

Daz I love fightin. (*Beat.*) Fuckin love it. Bein outnumbered. Goin somewhere horrible twenty-handed. Shittin yourself, knowin, fuckin knowin you're gonna get done when you get there. Not givin a fuck. (*Beat.*) I love it.

H It's on its arse now, the football. The firms an that. All the banning orders, the constant fuckin surveillance. (*Beat.*) It's not like it were.

Daz Maybe it's you that ain't like you were?

H I'm not like I were. But it were blokes my age who invented this fuckin scene. The clothes, the jibbin, everythin. (*Beat.*) When it first started it fuckin felt like we were doin somethin. (*Beat.*) It felt like you were stickin two fingers up to everybody. I mean, a moral panic's a moral panic, but for a while in the eighties when the government were crackin down. The law, the Tories, the FA, the fuckin lot of them. They could fuckin beat the miners an the dockers an the printers an the fuckin Labour Party, but they couldn't beat us. We could still go round the country wreckin the place every Saturday afternoon.

 Pause.

But now . . . it's a fuckin theme park. There's more camera crews than lads. Tired old men an kids, posturin. There's gonna be pensioner thugs soon.

 Pause.

Daz You still get a good row now an again.

H Not at England games. Hardly anyone has a go. Not a real go.

Daz The Germans have a go.

H Only in Germany.

Daz An the Dutch.

H Never rated the Dutch.

Daz You can't say the Dutch don't have a go. Feyernoord an Ajax are top boys.

H I'm not talking about their clubs. I'm talkin about them as a country. As a nation.

Pause.

I blame it on the clothes.

Daz The clothes?

H They can't get their fuckin clothes right, can they? (*Beat.*) If they can't get the clothes right, they shouldn't fuckin bother. (*Beat.*) The Dutch? That's a nation that should be able to have a right go. Urban. Industrial. Big fuckers. They like a drink. Hookers, hash, Heineken. The age of consent's twelve. Anythin fuckin goes. I understand all that, it's all good. (*Beat.*) But my question is this. How the fuck can it be such a progressive fuckin country when so many of their blokes are still tuckin their tops in their trousers? (*Beat.*) In this day an fuckin age? (*Beat.*) Don't get me wrong, I've tucked me top into me jeans in me time. An I know we're an island nation. Different an that. But fuck me. (*Beat.*) Same with the Germans. Tucked in. Mullets. Half-mast trousers. How the fuck can a whole country not get the length of their trousers right? (*Beat.*) I were in Düsseldorf durin the Euros in '88 An the Germans had a right go, an these mobs, the German ones, were full of the biggest fuckin blokes you've ever seen. Fuckin monsters. They came out the station, an all the England that were outside start backing off. I were shittin meself. But a few lads started laughin at them. Taking the piss about how they were all tucked in an their trousers were too short, laughin at these mad fuckin hairdos. An, you know, you start thinking, fuck, they're right. They looked fuckin shit. Tramps to a fuckin man. Some of them had, it weren't just their T-shirts, it were their sweaters tucked into their jeans, big fuckin belts, the lot. (*Beat.*) How the fuck can you be scared of someone who looks like that?

Pause.

Everyone just steams in an fuckin batters them . . .

Daz (*to H*) What's your favourite label then?

H I've always liked CP Company.

Daz Yeah.

H An I know Stoney gets a bad name cos it's everywhere, but if you leave the badge off they're still good. (*Beat.*) I like Paul Smith an all. It's good for me frame. Paul Smith's more for your skinnier lad. But then Paul Smith is a skinny bloke. When you put on a few pounds you should always go for Armani. He's a fat little cunt, so he knows where to put your paunch.

Daz I've always liked Prada.

H They're alright. But I don't like them tryin to do trainers. I fuckin hate fuckin fashion labels tryin to do trainers. They should leave it to the sportswear companies. (*Beat.*) Trainers are equipment. A pair of Stan Smiths beats a pair of Prada hands down.

Daz Aquascutum's good.

H I never got into that whole country gent thing. Deerstalkers an that. Every fucker walkin about lookin like the Duke of Kent. I once saw a bloke at a game in plus fours. He had on golf shoes, the fuckin lot.

Daz Give you a sore one with the spikes.

H Shit if you wanna do a runner. Break your fuckin neck.

34

Daz I like Lacoste.

H There's a big Lacoste place in town here. I was gonna check it out. The security on them's always shit. It's always just one little bird in the shop on duty. You almost feel bad about robbin them.

Pause.

Daz Never been into thievin myself.

H No. (*Produces a mobile phone.*) Lucky you.

Daz You'll never get a signal in here.

H Maybe you've never had to. Thieve. (*Looks at the phone.*) Hello moto. (*Takes the back off the phone, takes out a wrap and gives it to Daz.*) When I were your age. (*Beat.*) How old are you?

Daz (*begins to chop the wrap up*) Twenty-five.

H Younger, I were. There were fuck-all to do. Everythin were fucked-up. The recession. The north got fuckin destroyed. You had to go on the rob. Or fuck off somewhere. (*Beat.*) People were going abroad, to work, Germany, Spain, wherever, *Auf*-fuckin-*wiedersehen Pet*. But it were older blokes with trades workin on buildin sites. Lads my age didn't have trades. We couldn't do nothin. What the fuck use were we to anyone? We had to go on the rob.

Pause.

It isn't your fault where you're born. Manchester were a village till the Industrial Revolution. People only went there for work. When I were around there was fuck-all to do. (*Beat.*) Whenever there's too much of somethin, a surplus, you have to offload it, don't you? It's common fuckin sense. The more you have of somethin, the less it's worth. Basic fuckin supply an demand.

*Daz takes a small line of cocaine, leaving a far larger
line which he offers to H.*

When there ain't enough jobs then there's a surplus of
men. (*Beat.*) The most disruptive members of any society
are young males. The group, society, has to expel them.
To stay stable. (*Takes a line of cocaine.*) Look at China.
(*Beat.*) They're gonna be fucked in future. Too many
men. Not enough women. Why? You're allowed one
kiddie, yeah?

Daz (*chopping up more lines*) Yeah.

H None of them want girls. Women are no fuckin use.
Waste of time if you're a fuckin peasant havin a girl. You
chuck it away if it's a girl. Try again for a boy. Everybody
does it. (*Beat.*) Twenty, thirty, forty years down the line,
you end up with millions more men than women. You've
got all these blokes who can't get a woman, can't even
get a fuck. An they're all only-fuckin-childs. You know
what they're like at the best of times? (*Beat.*) You ain't an
only-child?

Daz (*takes another tiny line*) No.

H There's gonna be fuckin millions of them. Can't get
laid. Spoilt.

Daz (*offering H another huge line*) They're gonna go
crazy.

H Big fuckin trouble. (*Takes the line.*) What they gonna
do with them? How d'you get rid of them? Stick them in
the army? Send them abroad? Then it's the rest of the
world's fuckin problem. We used to do it. That's why we
had an empire. The empire were a dumping ground for
the people we didn't need. Too many poor. Too many
kids. Get rid of them. Empty the prisons. Australia.
Canada. New Zealand. South Africa. Anywhere'll fuckin
do.

Pause.

Our history. We're a country of criminals. Always have
been. Outlaws. The highwayman. Pirates. They're the
folk heroes of this country. (*Beat.*) You look back to
the Elizabethans . . . people are startin to explore the
unknown parts of the world. Some countries, they used
to send people out to convert the infidel. They were doin
it for God. Not us, though. This country was only ever
interested in the bottom line. Money. Goods an riches.
Trade an traffic. Merchandise. If we didn't get there first,
we stole it off whoever did. Elizabeth the first, Gloriana,
Good Queen Bess said the use of the sea and air is
common to all, neither can any title to the ocean belong
to any people or private man.

Pause.

Now what she were really sayin to all the other
privateers, slave-traders an pirates who were knockin
about the Atlantic coasts lookin for opportunities was,
knighthoods lads, knighthoods for one an fuckin all if
you get over there an rob the Spanish Main blind. It's not
thievin if it's from the enemy, it's patriotic.

Pause.

Lads like us, we've had to do the same thing. Fuck off.
Go abroad. Look for somethin to do. They fuckin hate
lads like us at home. The only time they need us is when
there's a war to be fought. We're the scum of the earth,
a disgrace to our country . . . but we ain't a burden. We
ain't signin on. We ain't beggin. We're on our bikes,
we're . . . The only reason there was an empire is because
lads like you an me were willin to go out there an put
ourselves about a bit. An if we had to crack a few heads
to get somewhere . . . Everywhere you go, you meet lads
like me. All over the world. In pubs, clubs, nicks. (*Beat.*)
You always meet lads like me in the nick.

Daz You done time all over then, H?

H (*takes a line of cocaine*) There is a corner of a foreign jail that is for ever England.

    Pause.

Daz When were you last at home?

H Not for a long fuckin time.

Daz What? Never?

    Pause.

H Once or twice.

Daz You ain't got a family?

    Pause.

H Yeah.

Daz Kids?

H No. (*Beat.*) I mean. You know . . . a sister.

Daz You ain't been married or nothin?

    H shakes his head.

Not even close?

    Pause.

H Once.

    Pause.

But it turned out she were a brass.

Daz That ain't so good.

H You gotta do what you gotta do. (*Beat.*) Same for women as men, ain't it?

Daz Yeah.

Pause.

H You gotta do what you gotta do.

Pause.

Daz So what sort of business are you on today?

Pause.

H (*lays back down on his bunk*) It's a long story, mate.

Pause.

Daz We ain't goin nowhere, are we?

Pause.

H I'm supposed to be meetin this bloke.

Daz A mate, is he?

H Yeah. (*Beat.*) Well, no . . . more a sort of partner. (*Beat.*) A business partner.

Daz An you work together?

H We did.

Daz Is he English?

H No. (*Beat.*) He's a scouser.

Daz What's a manc doin workin with a fuckin scouser? You fuckin hate each other, don't you?

H He's a grafter.

Daz Was that what went wrong?

H You gotta understand, mate. Club loyalty, any loyalty, you put it aside when you're workin. (*Beat.*) A pound's a pound. Don't matter where it comes from. All that matters is the score.

Pause.

Daz An he's a thief.

H What, you think cos he's a scouser he's gotta be a thief?

Daz No.

Pause.

H The Echo's a ticket tout. (*Beat.*) Or he was.

Daz The Echo?

H Yeah.

Daz Why d'you call him the Echo?

H He's a scouser, an when he's a bit stressed he repeats everythin you fuckin say. (*Beat.*) The Liverpool Echo.

Daz Well, that's a first, a scouser that ain't a thief.

H Don't get me wrong, he ain't averse to a bit of low-level larceny neither. I mean, you know, you don't wanna leave your life savings unattended when he's around. But he was mostly into tickets. An he's a good one. Big time, yeah. He taught me how it all works. He's got a bit of savvy. He saw the opportunity that was there when all the travel companies started usin touts to supply tickets for their football packages. So he started his own company. For your more discernin lad. Started runnin his own trips to the football, concerts, the whole lot. Went legit.

Daz That's the trick though. When to go legit. (*Beat.*) How to give it up.

H You think?

Daz You gotta give up sometime.

H Yeah, but once you're up an runnin. Once you're all legit, that's when you can start makin the real money. (*Beat.*) If you've got fifty screamin teenagers on a bus goin to see Take That in Rotterdam, then on its way back you can have fifty screamin teenagers an a coupla kilos of gak in one of the tyres.

Pause.

Same with the game, it's a great cover for smugglin. Thousands of English lads over. People flyin in from all fuckin points of the compass . . . Stuff goes back home, stuff goes down to the islands. (*Beat.*) You know what Customs are like? Lookin at the manifest for lads travellin alone. All of a sudden there's whole planeloads arrivin all over the place. An it's charters, so they fly at the worst times. If a couple of hundred blokes arrive at two in the mornin somewhere they don't go over the plane with the same diligence and professionalism, do they? They don't give a shit. The sniffer dogs just wanna get home an have a tin of Pedigree Chum. They just want to get you through so they can fuck off home.

Pause.

Daz I've been thinking that I wouldn't mind getting away somewhere for a holiday.

H Have you?

Daz Nothin like a bit of sun on your back, is there?

H Never been one for the beach.

Daz I quite fancy headin down to Ibiza or somethin.

H Ibiza.

Daz Yeah.

H You been down there before?

Daz Course. I've been a few times. (*Beat.*) It's alright.

Pause.

H I have to say, when I first went, '87 it were, I thought
. . . this'll never fuckin take off.

Pause.

Daz You missed the boat, then.

H Missed a big fuckin boat.

Pause.

It's all scousers run it down there.

Daz Is it?

H Yeah.

Daz Is your mate one of them?

H Bangkok's good too. Lots of lads out there. Lot of
Chelsea. (*Beat.*) Pattaya. Patpong on Sea. You can buy
anythin there, if you've got the money.

Daz It's havin the money's the problem. For goin away.

H Havin the money? Young lad like you. Fuck it, you
shouldn't need to worry about money. Just get out there
an jib it. I thought they teach you all that in the forces
anyway, livin up in the hills an skinnin rabbits an that.

Daz Fuck that. I wanna do it in style.

H I thought you said you weren't arsed about money?

Pause.

Daz D'you know what I'd really like to do?

H What's that?

Daz I'd like to own a boat. Just fuckin sail about the
place, no one to fuckin bother you. Must be great.

H Yeah.

Daz I love the sea. (*Beat.*) Buy a boat, hoist the Jolly Roger an sail the seven seas.

H I thought you didn't have any ambition?

Daz It's not an ambition, is it?

H It fuckin sounds like it.

Daz It's a fuckin dream. (*Beat.*) It's never gonna fuckin happen.

   Pause.

H I might be able to help you out there.

Daz What?

H If you wanna get away somewhere. Earn some proper money.

Daz You've already shown me the money.

H I'm not talkin about that fake stuff. Or fuckin sunglasses or watches, or any of that petty fuckin shit. (*Beat.*) I'm talkin about the chance for a really big score.

Daz Doin what?

H I dunno yet.

Daz You dunno yet?

H No.

Daz So how d'you know it's somethin big?

H He told me.

Daz Who told you?

H (*gets up and looks at Daz*) This bloke I'm meetin. The Echo. I got a letter from him in prison. Haven't heard from him in two years an I get a letter. Tells me he needs a favour. There'll be a good drink in it for you.

Daz What? He's gonna buy you a drink?

Pause.

H (*lays back down*) Well, if you ain't fuckin interested.

Daz No. Sorry, mate. (*Beat.*) C'mon. I am. I'm sorry. (*Beat.*) What does he want you to do?

Pause.

H (*sits back up*) He says, I've got to come over for the game. I wanna meet you. Have a catch-up an stuff. An I wonder if you can do one thing for me.

Pause.

I need three passports.

Daz An you can get passports?

H Course.

Pause.

Well, don't you get it?

Daz He needs a passport.

H Why does he need passports? (*Beat.*) He's fucked-up. He's lookin to disappear.

Daz You reckon?

H I know him. Somethin's happened. He's spooked. I dunno what, but he's fucked-up. The last time I see him he's doin great, better than fuckin great, then all of a sudden he needs a passport. From me. Why from me? (*Beat.*) There's plenty blokes at home can get him a passport. (*Beat.*) He wants it from me cause he don't want anyone at home knowin what he's up to. He needs to escape from somethin. Someone. (*Beat.*) It's gotta be somethin interestin.

Daz How d'you know?

H I just do. (*Beat.*) I've been doin this for years. I've never done anythin else, have I? (*Beat.*) I can smell a big score. I can fuckin smell it. (*Beat.*) That's why I was gonna ask you if you fancy comin along.

Daz Me?

H You said you fancy gettin away.

Daz Yeah.

H There's gonna be money to be made here. (*Beat.*) You could play it safe an you miss out or you can gamble an the next thing you know the next coupla years are taken care of.

    Pause.

Daz What would I have to do?

H Just come along an hang about. (*Beat.*) A bit of back-up.

Daz Back-up for what? (*Beat.*) You don't look like you need back-up to me.

H No?

Daz No.

H I told you, I don't do violence. (*Beat.*) I sub-contract the rough stuff.

    Pause.

I'm gonna go an meet him, find out what he's up to, then I'm gonna rip him off.

    Pause.

Daz Why would you rip him off?

H Come along an I'll tell you.

Pause.

Daz No. (*Beat.*) I'll pass.

H Why?

Daz Come on. (*Beat.*) I've known you two minutes an you tell me you're gonna rip off some bloke you've known for fuckin years? (*Beat.*) What if I come along an you rip me off?

H You think I'm gonna rip you off, mate? (*Beat.*) Fuckin Marine Commando? Fuckin trained killer?

Daz What were you tellin me about opportunity?

H You gotta take it when it comes.

Daz I'm an opportunity.

H You're not an opportunity. You ain't got any money in this. You got nothin to lose. (*Beat.*) I mean you gotta grab your opportunities when they come along.

Pause.

All it takes is bollocks.

Daz It ain't that I ain't got the bollocks.

H I wasn't sayin that.

Daz I hope not.

H I mean. If there's anythin history proves, it's that you need fuckin bollocks if you want to do anythin.

H You sure you don't wanna come along an see what happens?

Daz No.

H You don't even want some of the fake paper?

46

Daz Listen. I'll tell you what. Give me your number an when we get out an I'll go an meet my mates an then I'll give you a bell. (*Beat.*) We can maybe meet later for a beer.

H Can't do that, mate. You'll have to let me know now. This is happenin as soon as I get out of here.

Pause.

Daz I'm sure.

H Your're sure

Daz Yeah.

H It's your loss.

Pause.

You coulda done alright outta this.

Daz I'm sure I could. But I already told you I don't rip off me mates. (*Beat.*) I couldn't rip off a mate.

Pause.

H We used to be mates. (*Beat.*) We worked together a lot. (*Beat.*) In-fuckin-seperable at times, we were. But . . . (*Takes out the wrap and dabs the remainder of the contents.*) When I were in Denmark, inside, the last person I spoke to, before I got nicked, the last person I saw, was the Echo. (*Beat.*) I was in the hotel, he popped out. Next thing I know the door gets kicked in and I'm away.

Pause.

Now, I don't know whether it was down to him or not, what happened. He's maybe even comin here to try and make things right with me. But I ain't takin the risk. It's time for a little bit of compensation.

Pause.

If he's runnin, then he's weak. You take advantage of other people's weakness. You don't get angry, you wait for your opportunity. (*Beat.*) That's business, innit?

Daz That's revenge, mate. (*Beat.*) An what if he didn't do it? (*Beat.*) You don't know?

H That's the game, innit?

Pause.

So you're sure you don't wanna?

Daz I told you.

H Last-chance saloon?

Pause.

Daz It don't bother you that he's a mate?

Pause.

H There's a bloke, he's dead now. Robert Nozick. (*Beat.*) I take it you're not familiar with his work?

Daz I ain't, no.

H He was a Professor of Moral Philosophy. At Harvard. An he had this theory. Entitlement Theory. People are entitled to anything they acquire in a just way. An anything you acquire from someone who acquired it in a just way is justly acquired. Anythin which ain't has to be restored to their rightful owners. What he calls a justice-preservin transaction.

Daz Fuckin hell. You have done a lot of time.

H Now, what I say, and Nozick sort of agrees, is if everythin in the world, everythin, every fuckin single thing, was initially acquired by force, which it was . . . then all initial acquisitions are illegitimate. No fucker

48

legally owns anythin. An if they're unjustly acquired then they can be transferred in an unjust way. Now, if that ain't right, an it is legitimate to acquire things initially by force, then it must still be the same today.

Pause.

You just think that everythin you do is a justice-preservin transaction.

Pause.

Morally, you're at peace, because you concur with cutting-edge libertarian theory.

Daz Well, best of luck to you.

Pause.

How long were you in Denmark for?

H Two years.

Pause.

He fucked a lot of things up for me.

Daz You ain't worried he's settin you up again?

Pause.

H Maybe.

Pause.

But if I know Ray. *An I do.* (*Beat.*) It's all about beatin him to the punch.

Pause.

Daz Ray?

H Yeah.

Pause.

That's his name?

Daz Whose name?

H Ray.

Pause.

Sorry, yeah, the Echo.

Pause.

Ray Lee.

Pause.

Daz Ray Lee.

H Yeah.

Pause.

D'you know him?

Daz No. But I wouldn't mind one of his passports.

Pause.

I could do with a passport.

Pause.

H What d'you want a passport for?

Pause.

Daz Well, to be honest . . . I haven't really told you everythin, either.

H No?

Daz No.

H I knew you were up to summat.

Daz No you didn't.

H I did. I fuckin did. (*Beat.*) I'm tellin you, mate. I know when there's somethin goin on with someone. (*Beat.*) I know there's a score to be had here today. I can sense it. Same with you, mate. I just know with people. Soon as I met you I thought . . . I just knew.

Pause.

So what is it? (*Beat.*) On the run? CSA? Murder someone?

Pause.

Daz Thing is, havin been in an that . . . in the Marines. When you come out you stay on the reserve list. They can call you back up anytime. (*Beat.*) For ten fuckin years. (*Beat.*) I don't wanna get called up again. End up in Iraq. That's why I wanna fuck off for a while. Be on the safe side. I've done my bit.

Pause.

I'll come with you for a passport.

H That's all?

Daz Seein as how we don't know what's happenin with your mate. I mean it might be nothin.

H It ain't nothin.

Daz Well, if it's somethin, great . . .

Pause.

I'll come along if you give me a passport.

Daz puts out his hand. H hesitates, then extends his hand. They shake.

Blackout.

Act Two

A room in a city centre hotel. Twin beds, a television, a wardrobe, a desk and a chair. A door to a bathroom offstage. H and Daz enter the room. Daz is carrying a Head bag.

Daz This is alright?

H Yeah.

H goes to the wardrobe and opens it. There are clothes already inside. He pulls out a holdall and places it on the bed. He opens a drawer in the desk. He closes it and goes into the bathroom, switching on a light. Daz looks around. Thinks about sitting down. We hear H opening cupboards in the bathroom. Daz looks at the bathroom. He opens the drawer in the desk a crack and looks in. He closes it. He opens the wardrobe door a crack and looks in. He closes it just as H comes back into the room.

Daz (*puts his bag down*) You alright?

H crosses to a mirror on the wall. He pulls it away from the wall and a cellophane bag drops into his hand.

H I am now. (*Holds up the cellophane bag.*) That's why I always put my hotel key in left luggage. So if you do get nicked, no one can come round for a snoop. (*Beat.*) D'you wanna beer?

Daz I'm fine.

H Go on. Have one. I'm havin one.

H opens the mini-bar and pulls out two bottles of beer.

He briefly searches for the bottle opener. Finds it, opens one of the bottles and hands it to Daz.

Daz Cheers.

H Wanna glass?

Daz I'm alright.

H turns back to the mini-bar and opens his own bottle of beer. He pours the beer into a glass, takes a long drink from it, pours the rest of the bottle into the glass. He then takes a miniature from the mini-bar and pours it into the remainder of the beer.

H Fuckin parched.

Daz Yeah.

H Custody makes me thirsty.

Daz Yeah.

Pause.

H Sit down, then.

Daz sits on the edge of the bed. H sits down at the desk and picks up the cellophane bag which he starts to unwrap. He looks round at Daz.

H Want somethin to eat?

Daz Wouldn't mind.

H picks up a room-service menu from the table.

H Order what you like.

Daz reads the menu. H pours white powder from the cellophane bag.

Daz (*indicates the room*) Is this place five-star?

H Dunno. (*Looks around.*)

Daz It's nice.

H (*points to the menu*) Is the room service twenty-four-hour?

Daz looks at the menu.

I think you need twenty-four-hour room service to be five star.

Daz Finishes at midnight, it says here.

H (*looks at his watch*) Just missed it. (*Beat.*) Must be four-star. (*He throws the bag away.*) Don't wanna be too obvious. (*He takes a card from his wallet.*) Always stay in okay hotels, though. (*He begins chopping the powder into lines.*) If I've got the money. (*Beat.*) This lot, their places are all fuckin huge. No one pays a blind bit of notice whether you're comin or goin.

Pause.

Daz Why d'you get a twin?

H You what?

Daz The room. (*Beat.*) Why a twin an not a double?

H Oh yeah. Well, thing is right, if I bring a woman, well a brass, back here, I don't like sleepin in the bed I fucked her in.

Pause.

I dunno why. It's just me.

Daz Like wet kit, dry kit.

H Eh, yeah. (*Beat.*) Wet kit, dry kit. (*Takes the menu from Daz.*) Don't you want anythin?

Daz It finishes at twelve, mate.

H Ain't you hungry?

Daz I'm fuckin starvin.

H We could go down to the bar if you want. They'll do sandwiches or somethin. (*Takes a line.*) For fuckin residents.

Daz Yeah.

H drains his beer glass, stands up and crosses to the bed. He opens the holdall and pulls a vacuum-packed brick of money from it. Daz looks into the holdall.

H I told you there were plenty.

H goes to the wardrobe, opens it. He goes into the pocket of a jacket and pulls out a knife. He comes back to the bed slicing through the package of money he is holding. The notes fall onto the bed. He picks up a handful of money and gives it to Daz.

Daz How much is in each?

H Depends. (*He picks up one of the bundles of twenties and throws it to Daz.*) Four in the twenties.

Daz catches the bundle.

H An two in the tens.

Pause.

Daz So this is worth two?

H A grand if you're buyin it.

Pause.

Daz What about the passport?

H goes to the desk and pulls out a package that is taped underneath, which he unwraps and gives to Daz.

H You've got a choice.

Daz So I see. (*He looks at one of the passports.*) I dunno if I fancy bein a Belgian. (*He looks through the passport.*) These look pretty good. (*Beat.*) Where d'you get them?

H Brussels.

Daz They're really fuckin good.

H They're not fake. They're fuckin real. They're blanks. Stolen. See, Belgium, they issue them from town halls, so they're easy to steal. Terrorists' passport of choice. (*Beat.*) All they need is to be filled in an a photograph.

Daz Who'd have thought it? (*Beat.*) Belgium.

H Capital of Europe. Capital of fuckin crime. Makes sense, don't it? (*Beat.*) It's Albanians get the passports, they need them for the girls they smuggle.

Daz When we were in Kosovo, you could buy Albanian girls. They used to come round the bars hawkin them.

H Yeah. They don't strike me as being big on feminism.

　　Pause.

Mind you, they still have vendetta in Albania. Proper vendetta. An the thing with vendetta is, if a lad in one family kills someone, then the family of the lad who got topped get to kill any male relative of the killer. It's their right. The only place you can't be touched is in the house. All the men have to stay at home, an the women have to go to work.

Daz I wouldn't mind a bit of vendetta myself.

　　H sits at the desk. He bends down to take another line of cocaine. His mobile rings. H answers his phone.

H Hello.

　　Pause.

Yeah.

Pause.

A'right, mate.

Pause.

I'm sound.

Pause.

Where are you?

Pause.

In reception?

Pause.

Well . . .

Pause.

No.

Pause.

It's a bit . . .

Pause.

You're early.

Pause.

No. I ain't got a bird with me.

Looks at Daz.

Come up.

Pause.

Course not.

Pause.

Yeah.

Pause.

Five-two-five.

Pause.

Crackerjack.

Yeah. Crackerjack. (*Beat.*) Yeah. (*Beat.*) You come on up, mate. (*He puts the phone down.*)

Pause.

Come on up.

Daz Alright?

H Yeah.

H begins putting the money on the bed back in the holdall.

Daz Was that him?

H Yeah.

Daz How'd he sound?

H takes the money Daz is holding.

Daz (*keeps hold of the money*) Everythin alright?

H Yeah.

H pulls the money from Daz's hands and puts it in the holdall.

Daz You sure?

H (*gathers up the passports and puts them in the holdall*) Remember what I was tellin you about him? (*He zips up the holdall.*) He's got a bit of savvy. (*He puts the holdall in the wardrobe. He wraps up the passports and puts them in the wardrobe and closes the door.*) He can be a bit . . .

Daz Yeah.

H So you . . . we're . . . (*He indicates the wardrobe.*) . . . we're gonna have to be . . .

Daz Yeah.

H Don't say anythin. (*Beat.*) About anythin.

Daz I won't.

H Once I find out what's goin on. (*Beat.*) Until then, you don't know nothin.

Daz Yeah.

H You never say anythin till you know what's goin on.

    Pause.

Daz Listen. I can go if you want?

H No. No. Stay. Just . . .

    Pause.

He ain't gonna be expectin you.

Daz He ain't.

H So he might get a bit . . .

Daz Gotcha.

H Let me do the talkin. (*Beat.*) Don't worry about what I'm sayin. Or what he's sayin. Don't worry if it sounds a bit iffy or anythin. Just go along.

Daz Too late now, anyway.

    H goes back to the desk and snorts a long line. He goes to the mini-bar.

H You want another beer?

Daz I'm fine.

H pours most of a beer into his glass and tops it up with another miniature.

Daz (*to H*) You nervous?

H I'm fine.

Daz You're shakin.

H I ain't shakin.

Daz Fuckin hell, mate.

H I'm fine.

Daz Sit down.

H sits down. He takes a long drink. Looks at Daz. Takes a deep breath.

H I'm fine.

There is a knock at the door. H takes another long drink and puts down his glass. He checks the door of the wardrobe is fully shut. He goes to the door.

H Hello?

Ray Hello.

Pause.

It's me.

H Me?

Ray Me.

H Me?

Ray Me. (*Beat.*) It's me.

H Ray?

Ray Ray.

H (*to Daz*) Is there an echo in here?

Ray I'm out here.

H Echo?

Ray Echo.

H turns to Daz, stifling a laugh.

Ray Open the fuckin door, Hawk.

H opens the door a crack.

H Alright . . .

Ray pushes it open from the outside.

. . . mate.

Ray enters. He is in his mid-thirties, strongly built, similarly dressed to the others.

Ray What the fuck are you up to, makin me talk through a fuckin door?

H Can't be too careful.

Ray Who the fuck d'you think it was?

H Room service?

Daz Can't be.

Ray turns to Daz.

Daz It's not twenty-four-hour. (*Puts his hand out to Ray.*) Alright, mate.

H (*to Ray*) This is Daz.

Ray turns back to H.

Ray Daz?

H (*turns to Daz, then back to Ray*) Yeah.

Pause.

Ray (*turns to Daz then back to H*) An who the fuck is fuckin Daz?

H Him.

Ray Him.

Daz (*to H*) I see what you mean about the echo thing.

Ray (*to H*) Echo thing?

Daz laughs.

H I was tellin him about your nickname. The Liverpool Echo.

Daz (*goes to the mini-bar. To Ray*) Drink, mate?

Ray Not any more.

H You teetotal now?

Ray Liverpool Echo.

H Cause you repeat everythin an you're a scouser.

Ray Not any more.

Daz You ain't a scouser?

Ray I don't get called that any more, any more.

H Okay, okay.

Daz (*offers Ray a beer*) D'you make the game?

Pause.

Ray No. I didn't make the fuckin game.

Daz shrugs, sits down and opens the beer.

H Not really into football are you, Ray?

Ray Not England, anyway.

Daz (*to H*) That's typical scouse, innit.

Ray Is it?

Daz Foreign fuckin country.

H That's down to the Celtic influence, that.

Pause.

Thing about the Celts was. The reason they don't really figure in history. (*Beat.*) They never wrote anything down. It was an oral culture.

Pause.

So it disappeared.

Daz Tragic.

Ray (*to Daz*) Listen. I don't wanna be funny or anythin yeah?

Daz Yeah.

Ray But me an the Hawk here . . .

Daz Hawk?

Pause. To H.

Hawk?

H Yeah. Hawk.

Ray His name's Hawkins.

Pause.

He hasn't told you his name?

Daz H.

Ray H? (*to H*) So you're not the Hawk any more? (*Beat.*) You could have been a bit more imaginative couldn't you? (*Beat.*) I mean how many AKAs have you got?

H One or two.

Ray An you choose H? That's a bit obvious, mate. Come on. (*to Daz*) He's got plenty to choose from. (*to H*) Haven't you? (*Beat.*)

Pause. To Daz.

His older friends, people who've known him for a long time, who know what he's like, how he can spot a rabbit a fuckin mile off. They call him the Hawk.

Pause. To Daz.

So yeah. (*Beat.*) Me an the Hawk here, or H, we've got a bit of business to talk over, an it's a little bit . . .

H Sensitive . . .

Ray (*looks at H*) Yeah. (*Looks back at Daz.*) Sensitive. (*He goes over and stands in front of Daz.*) An I'm not into makin snap decisions on people or anythin like that. I'm not what you'd call a judgemental sort of person at all really. (*Beat.*) But seein as how I don't know who or what the fuck you are. I would be really fuckin appreciative if you would leave us the fuck alone for a few minutes.

Pause.

If you don't fuckin mind?

Pause.

Daz I don't fuckin mind.

Ray Cheers.

Daz But. I was doin a little bit of business with . . . the Hawk myself.

Ray Were you?

Daz Yeah. (*Beat.*) I was.

H (*to Ray*) Nothin major. Just a bit of a sideline. Nothin for you to be worryin about, mate.

Daz It's none of your fuckin business, in fact . . .

Pause.

Ray (*to Daz*) Tell you what. Fuck off out of it now and you can keep the beer.

Pause.

Daz (*stands up*) What I'll do is, I'll go downstairs and wait in the bar for you two girls to finish what you're doin.

H (*to Daz*) Yeah, mate. You do that.

Pause.

Daz (*to Ray*) Then I'll see you later.

Ray I can't wait.

Daz (*puts his bottle of beer down. To Ray*) An don't fuckin touch. (*Picks up his bag.*)

H You can leave that here if you want.

Pause.

Daz It's alright, mate. (*Looks at Ray.*) You dunno who's around, do you?

Daz exits.

Ray (*watches him go, turns to H*) What's fuckin goin on?

H What?

Ray Who the fuck is that?

H Daz.

Ray What the fuck is he doin here?

H He's alright.

Ray What's this fuckin bit of business, bit of business he's talkin about?

H It's nothin.

Ray Nothin?

H Yeah.

Ray It's always fuckin nothin with you.

Pause.

He better not know why I'm here.

H He doesn't. (*Beat.*) I don't know why you're here.

Pause.

He's nothin to do with you an me. (*Goes to the wardrobe and takes out the holdall. He unzips it and pulls out a bundle of the fake money.*) He wants to buy a bundle of fake paper.

Ray takes one of the notes and looks at it closely.

H (*goes to the table and chops out a line*) I have to make a livin. (*Beat.*) We can't all be respectable. (*He snorts a line.*)

H holds out the note he's snorted with to Ray. Ray ignores it and dabs a line directly from the table with his finger. Ray goes to the mini-bar and takes out a beer.

H An he could be useful.

Ray Useful?

H Yeah.

Ray How the fuck could he be useful?

Pause.

H He's a commando.

Ray A fuckin commando?

H Used to be.

Ray I told you not to bring anyone else into this.

H You told me not to bring anyone else into what?

Ray Why the fuck would you want to bring someone else in?

Pause.

I cannot fuck this up today.

H Can't fuck what up?

Ray An if anyone or anythin was to fuck it up for me . . .

H Fuck what up for you, Ray?

Pause.

Ray Where d'you meet him?

H In the nick.

Ray The nick?

H Yeah.

Ray What nick?

H A police station. Here.

Ray When?

Pause.

H Yesterday.

Pause.

Ray You got fuckin nicked yesterday?

H Yeah.

Ray How the fuck did you get nicked?

H It's an England game.

Pause.

Ray You sure he's not a bizzy?

H He's a football lad. (*Beat.*) I got nicked. He got nicked. We both got nicked.

Pause.

Then we got talkin.

Ray You got talkin?

H Yeah.

Ray As fuckin usual. (*Beat.*) An what d'you get talkin about? (*Beat.*) How to skin a rabbit? (*Beat.*) Arctic manoeuvres?

Pause.

H (*points to the note*) Money.

Ray Money. (*Looks at the note.*)

Pause.

These are quite good.

H I know.

Ray Where d'you get them?

H Copenhagen.

Pause.

There's euros too.

Pause.

Half face-value. (*Beat.*) If you want any?

Ray That's alright.

Pause.

You manage to sort the other thing out?

H takes the bundle containing the passports out of the bag.

Thank fuck.

H unwraps the bundle and gives it to Ray.

Cheers, mate. You dunno how grateful I am.

Pause. Looks at the passports.

Belgian?

H Or South African.

Pause.

Ray Great.

H Paedophile or racist. (*Beat.*) The choice is yours.

Pause.

Ray Could you not have got me somethin more exotic?

H The only other countries who don't look after their passport distribution are Italy and Argentina.

Ray I wouldn't a minded bein an Argie.

H Oh yeah, you look really Argentinian. (*Beat.*) An seein as how you don't speak Italian . . .

Ray Fuckin Afrikaans it is then.

Pause.

Good to see you, Hawk.

H (*nods and takes a drink*) Good to see you, kaffir.

Ray (*hands the note back to H and sits down*) Sorry, mate.

H What for?

Ray Just now. (*Beat.*) When I come in. You know . . .

H S'alright.

Ray I'm a bit fuckin tense. (*Beat.*) You don't know who's around, do you?

Pause.

H How d'you come over?

Ray I drove.

H You fuckin drove?

Ray (*drinks*) Yeah. (*Continues to look through the passports.*) These are spot-on, by the way.

H Yeah.

Ray Quality.

H They're not fakes, neither.

Ray No.

H They're the real thing. (*Beat.*) Blanks. Stolen to order.

Ray Fuck.

H Only the best for you, Ray. (*Takes the passports back.*) All you need to do is fill it in with the name of your choice an your photo an you're away.

Pause.

You thought of a name, have you?

Ray shakes his head.

H If you'd gone for the Belgian I was gonna suggest Tintin.

Ray (*takes a large bundle of cash from his pocket*) How much did we agree?

Pause.

H I don't think we did agree . . . did we?

Ray Didn't we?

H No.

   Pause.

Ray (*smiles*) Same old Hawk. (*Beat.*) Have I got to haggle? (*Beat.*) I'm sure there's some fuckin Arab blood in you somewhere. (*He counts out some money.*) It was five weren't it? (*He holds the money out.*)

   Pause.

H (*puts the passports back in their wrapping*) Let's just agree that you tell me what the fuck's goin on here today. Then we'll talk about a price.

Ray You know what's happenin.

H The truth.

   Pause.

Ray Do one. (*He puts a bundle of money on the table.*) That's the money there. Five grand.

   Pause.

Take it.

H (*puts the passports in his back pocket*) You're not having them till you tell me what's goin on.

Ray Tell you what's goin on?

   Pause.

What's fuckin wrong with you?

H Come on, Ray. I'm not fuckin stupid. There's somethin goin on here today an I wanna know what.

   Pause.

Ray I'm here to get the passports.

H If you want them, you're gonna have to tell me.

Ray (*laughs*) Piss off.

H I'm fuckin serious.

Pause.

Ray Well, I won't fuckin bother then.

H Well, no fuckin passports then.

Ray (*stands up*) Well, I'll fuckin go then. Yeah?

H Okay.

Ray moves towards the door.

You'll just have to take your chances back home.

Ray stops.

Sit down.

Pause.

Ray (*sits*) Listen.

Pause.

Hawk. (*Beat.*) H. (*Beat.*) Mate.

H Things not been goin so great for you at home?

Pause.

Ray Things fuck-up, H.

H I thought you'd cracked it?

Ray Yeah.

H What about the tickets?

Ray I'm tellin you, mate, the internet's destroyed the touting business. Only the big tournaments are any use. That fuckin e-Bay shite killed us all stone dead.

H Fuckin e-Bay?

Ray The internet.

H What the fuck has that got to do with anythin?

Ray What the fuck has it to do with anythin? (*Beat.*) Click of the fuckin mouse an everyone's a fuckin market-trader now. You take away a man's fuckin right to manipulate the price an what's he got left?

H You must be slippin.

   Pause.

Ray We're all okay when we're rolling along, happy as fuck, an then . . . things go wrong, somethin falls through, somethin don't work out an you end up back on the bones of your arse again.

H (*laughs*) You should have stuck a bit away for a rainy day then, shouldn't you?

Ray Well I didn't, did I?

   Pause.

H What's really happened?

   Pause.

Did one of your little smugglin trips go wrong? (*Beat.*) The wheel fall off the bus or somethin?

   Pause.

Tell me. (*Beat.*) Lose someone's gear an piss them off?

Ray We both lost someone's gear, remember?

H I've had two years to remember.

   Pause.

D'you know anythin about that?

73

Pause.

Ray What? (*Beat.*) You think I had somethin to do with that?

H I dunno. (*Beat.*) You walk out the door an the next minute the room's full of the local drugs squad.

Pause.

Ray An why would I do that?

Pause.

Hawk. (*Beat.*) Come on. When somethin goes wrong. It's every man for himself.

Pause.

Denmark was a fuck-up. I fucked-up. You fucked-up.

Pause.

We both got fucked-up.

H How did you get fucked-up?

Ray How did I get fucked-up?

Pause.

Hawk. (*Beat.*) What the fuck d'you think happened when I went home?

Pause.

I know you got time. An I know you kept your mouth shut. But I had to go back home an fuckin tell them the gear was gone . . . an you know how that works?

Pause.

There's no fuckin bad luck, better luck next time. (*Beat.*) It's where's our fuckin gear? Where's our fuckin money?

Pause.

An they're not interested in knowing it's mouldering on a shelf in the evidence store of the police HQ in wunderbar, wunderbar Copen-fuckin-hagen.

Pause.

Where's our fuckin money?

Pause.

I had to give them the business, Hawk. No more fuckin businessman, fuckin boss, Ray. I'm a fuckin employee. I have to do what I'm told. (*Beat.*) They said okay, you're the ticket lad. You can run the business for us as a front.

Pause.

How the fuck d'you think I ended up in all this shit?

Pause.

An I had to fuckin cover for you. Your fuckin track record. (*Beat.*) They were all for fuckin gettin you done when you were inside just in case you'd ripped them off. It was all I could fuckin do to convince them you'd done fuck-all.

Pause.

You dunno what it's like, H. These fuckers, they get their fuckin claws into you an you're fucked. They fuckin take over everythin. It's fuckin not just oh we're gonna be usin your coach goin over to here or there now an again, they take over your fuckin books, they take over the whole fuckin business. They don't give a shit. They've got corner-shops turnin over half a million quid a week. Hairdressers in some back street takin in more money than a fuckin supermarket. (*Beat.*) There's no, eh actually lads, you know what, I think we might be attractin a little bit of attention here. They're not takin any grief. Everyone's on my back. Inland Revenue, Customs and Excise. Fuckin Interpol . . .

Pause.

You don't do it, you're fuckin dead. You say anythin, you're dead. You let them get on with it, the law get you. (*Beat.*) So you're fuckin right I'm disappearin. If I don't disappear one way, I'll be disappearin another way. (*Chops out a couple of lines on the table.*) An the fuckin shite thing is. (*He takes one of them.*) It's a fuckin shite time to be fuckin leavin. It's fuckin boom-town at home just now. (*He takes the other one.*)

H (*joins him*) Go easy. Leave some for the rest of us.

Ray (*rubbing his nose*) Well, it's a special occasion isn't it?

H Give yourself a fuckin heart attack.

Ray takes another line.

Fuck's sake. (*Beat.*) What are you so nervous about?

Ray What am I so nervous about?

H Yeah.

Ray I just fuckin told you.

H It can't be that bad. (*Takes a line.*)

Ray Can't be that fuckin bad?

Pause.

Are you not fuckin listenin?

Pause.

Listen. (*Beat.*) This isn't just some little local firm I'm dealin with here. (*Beat.*) There's a lot of international investment around now. International investment. (*Beat.*) A lot of outside influence. (*Beat.*) D'you get me? (*Beat.*) From over the water.

Pause.

This is the fuckin bhoys we're talkin about here.

Pause.

The fuckin Provos.

Pause.

PIRA.

Pause.

H Fuckin hell.

Ray Fuckin hell is right.

H Why'd you get involved with those lads?

Ray Well it's kinda difficult not to these days. (*Beat.*)
Since the ceasefire a lot of them have been at a loose end.
They're not all in Colombia just to show them how to
make fuckin car bombs, you know.

Pause.

An from what I seem to remember at the very fuckin
beginnin it was your fuckin idea that we got involved in
smugglin. I just wanted to run a fuckin legit company.

Pause.

H If you're disappearin an these fuckers have left you
fuckin potless . . . (*Beat.*) How the fuck are you gettin the
money to run?

Pause.

It's today, isn't it?

Pause.

Tell me.

Long pause.

Ray I've gotta meet this bloke.

H What bloke?

Ray I dunno him.

H What are you meetin him for?

Ray I dunno.

H You must know summat.

Ray I don't.

H So you came over here to meet someone you don't know, about nothin?

Pause.

What you meetin him about?

Pause.

Ray I've gotta take him back home with me.

H Who is he?

Ray I dunno. (*Beat.*) He's comin from Amsterdam.

H Well, it not's just him you're takin home, then?

Pause.

Ray It might be a little bit of gear. I dunno.

H They wouldn't send you over here for a little bit of gear.

Pause.

This is a big score today, Ray. You're plannin on givin him the slip, fuckin off with the gear, an that's you gone.

Pause.

Ray There might be somethin in it. I dunno.

H (*laughs*) I fuckin knew it.

Ray You need to give me a chance to find out.

Pause.

H Have you spoke to him?

Ray Not yet. (*Beat.*) I've got to give him a phone.

H When?

Ray Soon as.

H Is he gonna be on his own?

Ray I dunno.

H What you plannin on doin?

Ray I'm plannin on doin nothin at the moment because I don't know enough about what the fuck's goin on. (*Beat.*) An you aren't fuckin helpin things by turnin up with fuckin Action Man there.

Pause.

H I've been thinkin . . .

Ray Well, don't you start thinkin. The last thing I fuckin need is your thoughts on anythin.

H We can do this together.

Ray Oh yeah, I'm gonna swan up with you an go, 'Oh by the way, me mate's comin with us.'

Pause.

He's gonna suss straight off.

H No. That's where this Daz kid comes in.

Ray Fuck that.

H We let him get the courier out of the way an we slip away with the gear.

Pause.

I mean, you're not gonna do him, are you? When the fuck did you last have a fight?

Pause.

Ray An what happens to him?

H Daz?

Ray Yeah.

H Fuck him.

Ray Fuck him.

H We tell him we'll fuckin meet him somewhere an fuck off.

Pause.

Ray D'you trust him?

H Don't be daft. (*Beat.*) He's a fuckin meat-head. A cockney casual. (*Beat.*) He's perfect. Nothin to do with us. He don't know anyone.

Ray How d'you know?

H He's just come out the army. (*Beat.*) He's a fuckin doorman, for fuck's sake. (*Beat.*) Fuckin knuckle-dragger.

Ray I'm not worried about his brains, I'm fuckin worried about him bein an ex-fuckin-commando.

Pause.

H They've all got eight pints of blood.

Pause.

Listen. I fed him a load of bollocks about graftin. How the money's good. How he can make a bit an fuck off round the world. He's fuckin desperate not to go back home.

Ray I know the fuckin feelin.

H He's on the fuckin reserve list. He's fuckin shittin it that he'll be getting called back up, end up in Iraq. (*Beat.*) He wants to disappear for a while till it all blows over. He's practically on the fuckin run.

Pause.

We offer to cut him in an then we take care of him.

Pause.

Ray An how do we do that?

H lifts his shirt so Ray can see the gun.

What the fuck is that?

H It's a gun.

Pause.

Ray A fuckin gun?

Pause.

Have you gone fuckin mental? (*Beat.*) A fuckin gun?

Pause.

You're goin fuckin soft, lad.

H You gotta risk a killin to make a killin.

Pause.

Ray You gotta fuckin what?

Pause.

We're not fuckin gangsters, Hawk. I know fuckin gangsters. (*Beat.*) We're a coupla spivs. (*Beat.*) A fuckin gun? They'll take that off you an shove it up your arse before you get the fuckin safety catch off.

Pause.

I dunno what it is, mate, what the fuck's wrong or what. You should maybe leave off the Tartan.

Pause.

Just let me pay you for the passports an go, Hawk.

Pause.

Please.

Pause.

I've got too much at stake here.

H You owe me.

Ray I cannot fuck this up today. An I cannot have you fuckin it up for me. (*Beat.*) I can't believe I'm standin here listenin to you.

Pause.

You're gonna fuck everythin up.

H Just like you fucked things up for me?

Ray What the fuck have I ever fucked-up for you?

H Two fuckin years inside in Denmark. (*Beat.*) Where the fuck am I after two fuckin years? Back at fuckin square one. Havin to start all over again. Goin round scroungin an askin for favours off of nobodies.

Ray We've all gotta ask for favours sometimes.

H Yeah. (*Pats his back pocket.*) It's me that's got your future here, in me fuckin pocket, just you fuckin remember that.

Ray Yeah.

Pause.

But you remember this, it's not just my future.

H Isn't it?

Ray No.

   Pause

Why do you think I need three passports?

H Coverin your arse.

Ray It's not just me, Hawk.

   Pause.

Not any more.

   Pause

H What? (*Beat.*) D'you get fuckin married?

   Pause.

Ray Yeah. (*Beat.*) I did.

   Pause.

H Fuck off.

Ray I did.

   Pause.

H (*laughs*) So that's why you're so fuckin spooked?

   Ray nods.

Fuckin hell, Ray.

   Pause.

Ray I've got a kid, an all. (*Beat.*) A little boy.

H Fuckin brilliant. (*Beat.*) What have you been tellin me all these years?

   Pause.

You can't afford to get fuckin attached to people.

Ray Yeah.

H Didn't you always tell me that?

Ray I need to tell you somethin else.

H No ties. Nothin you can't walk away from.

Ray I need to tell you somethin else.

H Yeah, you fuckin do.

Pause.

Ray When I got back from Denmark . . .

Pause.

Thing is . . . it was a fuckin mess.

Pause.

Everyone was in bits. I mean, they knew you were a wide boy. But they didn't know about the gear.

Pause.

It was a big shock . . . to everybody . . .

H What the fuck are you on about?

Pause.

Ray I'm on about your family.

Pause.

H What the fuck has my family got to do with any of this?

Ray At the end of the day, Hawk, that's all we've got.

H What?

Ray When it comes down to it.

Pause.

When it comes to the crunch. When things are fucked-up.

Pause.

It's your family.

Pause.

I got married . . . to Jackie.

Pause.

H Our Jackie?

Ray Yeah.

Pause.

I dunno what I would have done without her. I couldn't
see a way out.

Pause.

But she's like you, isn't she? (*Beat.*) There's always a way.

Pause. He takes out a photo from his pocket.

You gotta little nephew too. (*He gives the photo to H.*)
He's great.

Pause.

H Where are you goin?

Ray Bangkok.

H Bangkok?

Ray First like. Then, I dunno, on to Australia. Maybe.

Pause.

H An what you gonna do?

Ray Fuck knows. (*Beat.*) We'll find somethin. Maybe get
a bar somewhere. On a beach. (*Beat.*) You could come
with us?

Pause.

We were gonna let you know once we were all settled anyway.

Pause.

I didn't have to come here. I don't need all this hassle. (*Beat.*) I come to you to try and make things right.

There is a knock at the door. Nobody moves. There is another knock. H goes to the door. He opens it. Daz enters the room.

Daz (*to H*) Everythin alright?

Pause.

H Sound.

Ray (*to Daz*) I thought you got told to wait?

Daz (*looks up.* I did, yeah. (*Puts his bag down on the floor.*) But I got a little bit fed up. (*Beat.*) Waitin.

Pause.

I wouldn't mind another beer, H. (*to Ray*) The bar was shut downstairs. Apparently there was a football match on or somethin, an they didn't want any trouble.

H Yeah. (*Beat.*) Let's all have a beer, shall we?

H goes to the mini-bar. He takes out three bottles and opens them. Daz takes one. Ray shakes his head.

Daz You two been catchin up?

Ray Somethin like that.

H (*to Daz*) I was tellin Ray about you bein in the army. (*Beat.*) Tell him about when you was in the army.

Daz I wasn't in the army.

H You said you were a commando?

86

Daz Yeah. (*Beat.*) I was.

Pause.

H So what you on about?

Pause.

Ray (*to H*) Marines is navy.

Daz (*to Ray*) That's right, Ray.

Pause.

Ray (*to Daz*) Listen, mate. Sorry about earlier. I was a little bit tense. You know how things are? You never know who's around, do you?

Daz turns away.

H That's the one thing I feel I've missed out on, you know, the one place there's a gap in my education.

Daz What's that?

H Military trainin. (*Beat.*) I wouldn't have a clue how to fire a gun.

Pause.

Never even learned a martial art.

Daz I reckon the chop socky's overrated.

Pause.

Stick them in with a good boxer. It's punchin power that wins fights. Every time.

Pause.

Ray (*to Daz*) You box, do you?

Daz I did. (*Beat.*) Still train an have a spar an that. Nothin serious.

Ray Any good?

Daz I was alright.

Ray What weight?

Daz Welterweight.

Stands up and stretches his arm out to its full reach towards Ray. When his hand reaches Ray's face he curls it into a fist.

I've got a long reach too. For a welterweight. (*Beat.*) I can always keep myself out of trouble.

H (*beckons Ray over to the desk*) Get some of this down you. C'mon.

Daz (*to Ray*) You been in any trouble lately, Ray?

Ray takes another large line of cocaine. As he bends over the desk, H signals to Daz to calm down.

H Don't be daft. Ray's a respectable businessman now. (*Beat.*) Family man. (*Beat.*) He's in the fuckin Rotary Club.

Ray (*to H*) Fuck off.

H Well, you are, aren't you?

Pause.

(*to Daz*) He's got a mock Tudor mansion on the Wirral. (*to Ray*) Tell him about the good life, mate.

Pause.

Daz (*to Ray*) What sort of business are you in, then?

Ray I'm in the travel business.

Daz The travel business?

Ray Yeah.

Daz What? (*Beat.*) Taxi firm? Bus company? Airline?

Ray (*to H*) Confident, isn't he?

H (*nods*) That's the forces for you, mate.

Daz (*to Ray*) So how is it at the moment? The travel business?

Ray It's alright.

Daz (*to Ray*) How come you need to be here, then?

Ray Well, you know how it is in business. You gotta take your opportunities when they come along. No point in passin up the chance to make a bit of cash.

Daz An there's a lot of cash at stake today, is there?

Ray You think I'd come all this way for a dozen tickets an a couple of snide shirts?

Daz It's just H had the impression you were over here runnin away from somethin?

Ray Did he?

Daz Yeah.

    Pause.

Ray I think he must have gotta hold of the wrong end of the stick.

H Yeah. I got a bit ahead of myself there, maybe.

Ray He's got a bit of an overactive imagination.

    Pause.

Daz So you don't need those passports, then?

Ray (*looks at H*) They're for a friend.

    Pause. To Daz.

I hear you're maybe havin to get away from somethin at home yourself?

Daz I hear you do a bit of smugglin?

Ray Do you?

Daz Yeah. H told me.

Ray (*looks at H*) H. (*to Daz*) H always talks a lot.

    Pause.

That's been his biggest problem all these years. He tells people too much. (*Beat.*) You'll find that out sometime.

H I didn't hear you complainin much when we used to do the tickets. It's cos I open my mouth that we had the contacts.

Ray Goin in fuckin pubs an tellin everyone our business.

H Used to make Brewster's with my contacts. (*to Ray*) Tell him. Tell Daz how much money this mouth could make you. (*Beat.*) That time in France at the World Cup a lad I got to know in the Chinese Embassy got us the whole fuckin official allocation of tickets for the People's Republic of China Football Association.

Ray Well, yeah, that was a good one.

H For a grand.

Ray I'll give you that.

H We got rid of them the next day for twenty.

Ray Nineteen grand from havin a cup of coffee with a cufflink.

H Cause I were willin to open my mouth.

    Pause.

Ray (*to Daz*) So you wanna get involved in a little bit of business then, do you?

Daz That's why I'm here.

Ray Well, I hope you know what we're talkin about here. (*Beat.*) You know what you're gettin into?

Daz I think so.

Ray You think so? (*Offers a line to Daz.*)

Daz No thanks.

Ray I hope you're not opposed to drugs or anythin, are you? I know some of you soldiers can be a bit like that. My body's a fuckin temple an all that bollocks.

    Pause.

You don't wanna get out of your depth.

    Pause.

Daz I ain't never felt out of my depth. Nowhere.

Ray Glad to hear it.

    Pause.

Daz (*to Ray*) You ever feel out of your depth, Ray?

H Only when he's at the Rotary Club. (*to Ray*) If only they knew how you made your money. Fuckin hell.

Daz I know how you made your money, Ray.

Ray Do you?

Daz Yeah.

Ray Well, all the greats make the first bit of their fortune illegally.

H (*goes over to Ray and grabs his shoulder*) So how does it feel to be back slummin it with the lads? (*He rubs the material of Ray's jacket.*) You're still keeping up with the clothes, at least.

Ray I always liked me clobber.

H You did, didn't you? Very smart.

Ray When your club's King's of Europe . . . however many times is it now, H?

H gives Ray the finger.

There's a lot of shops to be robbed. (*Beat. To Daz*) Not that I rob shops any more.

H (*to Daz*) He was a right fuckin lefty firebrand too. Used to always be givin it the fuckin economic-refugee shit when we were runnin round bein vagabonds. (*Beat.*) Had a right romantic view of what he was up to. He thought he was the fuckin Robin Hood of import and export.

Ray (*line of cocaine*) Import and export. It's what made our country great.

Daz (*to H*) We were talkin about that.

H Outlaws.

Daz Pirates.

Ray (*to Daz*) Was he giving you his spiel, was he? (*Beat.*) Fuckin pirates. Walter fuckin Raleigh. Useless cunt. Tobacco. Potato. Great. But how the fuck did he miss the coca plant? (*Beat.*) An they fuckin knighted him. They should have fuckin hung the cunt.

Daz They did, didn't they?

H If he'd found it, it'd be legal an we'd be out of a fuckin job.

Ray Biggest business in the world. Bigger than food. An it's fuckin illegal. (*Beat.*) Fuckin madness. (*Snorts a line.*) You can't blame people though, can you? (*Beat.*) It's fuckin good gear.

Pause.

There's an argument that this is a social service. Every war the poor are fightin on this planet's funded by this stuff. Get along to your dealer an a slice of your money'll find its way back to whatever low-level insurgency is armin itself by doin a bit of this. Sendero Luminoso, FARC, Commando Vermelho.

Ray (*to H*) The Provos.

H You don't buy it, it's the dispossessed who suffer. (*He snorts one of the lines.*) There's nothin that puts the shite up the right like the white, is there?

Daz So if you ever get caught, are you gonna claim you're a political prisoner?

H I didn't. Last time.

Pause.

Daz Why d'you give it up, Ray?

Ray Everyone has to give up sometime.

Daz H ain't.

Ray Fuck that. Runnin around like a twenty-year-old for the rest of your life. (*Beat.*) That's no fuckin life. Takin advantage. Seein everyone as an opportunity. Rippin them off. Runnin away. Movin on. (*to H*) You're gonna get stuck for places to run one day, lad.

H Not while I've got these passports I won't.

Pause.

Daz You know your problem, Ray? You've gone fuckin soft.

Ray I've gone fuckin soft?

Daz I reckon, yeah. (*Beat.*) That's your fuckin problem. Playin fuckin golf with the fuckin Rotary Club. Sittin in your big fuckin house with your big fuckin wife an kiddie. You haven't got the bollocks for this now.

Ray stands up and moves towards Daz. H gets between Ray and Daz.

H (*to Daz*) He hasn't gone soft.

Daz No?

H (goes*to Ray*) Tell him about our plan for the bloke you're meetin.

Ray Do we have a fuckin plan?

H Tell him. (*to Daz*) He's meetin this bloke. An there might be a bit of gear involved. I'm not a hundred-percent sure yet, but we think we're gonna rob him.

Pause.

Daz (*to H, indicating Ray*) So that's what he's up to today?

H Yeah.

Daz (*to Ray*) Rob him of what?

H Of whatever gear he's got on him.

Daz (*to Ray*) How d'you know he's got gear on him?

H He's comin from the Dam.

Pause.

Daz Where you meetin him? At the airport?

Ray No.

Daz Where?

Ray I dunno.

H He's supposed to be takin him back home.

Daz How you gettin back?

H He's drivin.

Daz With him?

H Yeah.

Daz A bit risky, innit?

H (*to Daz*) I think they're settin him up.

Daz It sounds like it, don't it? (*to Ray*) I think you're gettin set up for a fall here, Ray.

H You're the fuckin sacrificial lamb, mate.

Daz They've gotta give someone up every now an again.

Pause. To Ray.

Is he from home, Ray? The bloke.

Pause.

Ray I think so.

Daz D'you know him?

Ray No.

Pause.

Daz An you reckon it's gonna be worth your while?

H Oh yes.

Daz (*to Ray*) Gonna give you enough to disappear is it?

Pause.

Maybe.

Daz You obviously haven't gone soft, mate.

Pause.

Okay. I'll help you. (*Beat.*) What d'you want me to do?

H Ray's supposed to be meetin him, but we're gonna phone him an get him to come here. We just need a distraction.

Daz A distraction?

H A physical distraction. We slip away.

Pause.

Daz I think I can manage that.

H We meet back here.

Ray No, not back here.

H No.

Ray No.

Pause.

Daz So what's in it for me?

Pause.

H What d'you want?

Pause.

Daz Three-way split.

Ray No fuckin way.

H Fair's fair, Ray. He's takin the same risks as us.

Ray No he fuckin isn't. No one's doin anythin until I find out what's happenin.

Pause.

Daz (*to Ray*) You'd be fucked, then, if this mob thought you'd rob them.

Ray They'd kill us.

Pause.

Daz No. They'd kill you. It's nothin to do with H. No one knows he's here.

Ray I do.

Pause.

An put it this way, if it fucks up an they're killin me, I'll make sure they'll be killin him. (*Beat.*) In fact, don't they already want to kill you, H?

Daz I can't imagine anyone wantin to kill H.

Ray (*to Daz*) No?

Pause.

You'd be surprised, then. (*to H*) Wouldn't he?

Pause.

There's loads of people want H dead. (*Beat. To H*) Haven't you told him about the amount of people you've fucked off over the years? Fuckin double-cross anyone. Rob his granny for ten bob. (*Beat.*) An always comin out of prison an settin up some mug for a fall. (*to Daz*) He makes a habit of that.

Daz I better watch myself, then.

Ray Yeah you better. (*Beat.*) An just remember, I'll be fuckin watchin you too.

Pause.

Daz (*to H*) You two didn't meet inside, did you?

Ray (*to Daz*) No, mate. I'm no mug.

H Ray don't go inside. Do you, Ray?

Pause.

Not Ray.

Pause.

Ray an prison don't go.

Pause. To Daz.

He's very careful is our Ray.

Daz I suppose you have to be. In the travel business.

H (*laughs*) Or is it luck? (*Beat.*) Yeah, maybe that's it.
Maybe he's just lucky.

Pause.

What's your secret, Ray? (*Beat.*) You careful, or lucky?

Pause.

Ray I'm lucky.

Pause.

That isn't a crime, is it?

Pause.

Daz (*to Ray*) H don't seem to have much luck.

Ray He's always been an unlucky fucker.

Daz The amount of fuckin time he's done.

Ray Yeah. (*Beat.*) An you gotta watch cos it can rub off,
his bad luck.

Daz It hasn't rubbed off on you. (*Beat.*) Stroke of luck he
met that Danish bloke or you wouldn't have your passport.
(*Beat.*) Stroke of luck he was in there in the first place.
Stroke of luck you didn't get fucked-up too.

Pause.

Ray (*to H*) What the fuck's he on about?

Daz What am I on about?

Ray Yeah.

Daz I'm on about how important it is that there's no fuckin person here today who's gonna end up havin all the good luck.

Pause.

No fuckin surprises.

Ray I've had enough fuckin surprises today.

H Me too.

Daz We stick together, we all get lucky.

Pause. To Ray.

What if he's tooled up?

Ray shrugs and gestures towards H.

H (*to Daz*) The town's full of different English firms, ain't it?

Daz Yeah.

H Pretend you know him. Or you recognise him.

Daz What, from football?

H Yeah. You just go, 'A'right, mate. (*Beat.*) Don't I know you?'

Ray 'Eh, I don't think so.'

H 'No, I do.'

Ray 'I don't think so.'

H 'I do. I do know you.'

Ray He'll be like clockin you, goin, 'Oh shit, who the fuck is this?'

H 'I remember now. You cut my cousin at Millwall last year. (*Throws a punch.*) Bang. (*Beat.*) Oh, no, sorry, it weren't you.'

H and Daz laugh.

Ray (*to H*) Or he could just go up an ask him the time.

Pause.

Daz (*to H*) What if he's tooled up?

H pulls the gun from under his shirt. He hands it to Daz.

Daz I thought you didn't like getting guns? (*Checks the barrel and the magazine.*) Nice. (*Hands it back to H.*)

H Yeah.

Daz Swiss.

Pause.

H Yeah.

Daz Whoever said they could only make cuckoo-clocks was a fuckin liar. (*Beat.*) Compulsory military service too, you know, the Swiss. Everybody. Like Israel. (*Beat.*) They make good fuckin guns. Suppose they need good guns to protect all the money. (*Beat. To Ray*) Everybody has to protect their money. (*Beat.*) Don't they?

Pause.

Alright. Let's do it. Phone him.

Ray What?

Daz Phone the bloke. Come on. Let's do this, if we're doin it.

Ray looks at H. Pause.

H (*to Ray*) Yeah. Come on. The quicker we do it, the quicker we'll be in a bar on a beach somewhere.

Ray gets his phone out and dials.

Daz Goin on holiday are we, lads?

H (*goes to take some cocaine*) Thinkin about it.

*Daz's mobile begins to ring. Ray looks at his phone,
confused. Daz holds up his phone. Daz knocks Ray to
the floor with a punch. Ray lies, dazed.*

Daz H. (*Beat.*) H. (*Beat.*) Stay calm. (*Beat.*) Don't do
nothin. Okay. (*Beat.*) Stay fuckin calm.

H What the fuck you doin?

Daz (*pulls Ray to his feet and sits him on the bed*) Stay
calm.

H What the fuck are you doin?

Daz (*searches Ray*) Trust me, H. Okay. I'm helpin you
out here.

*Daz takes Ray's car keys and a roll of money from his
pockets. He pulls a car-park ticket from another
pocket. He examines it. He puts the keys, the money
and the ticket in the pocket of his jacket.*

Daz You gotta trust me for the next couple a minutes.
Okay. (*Beat.*) I'm with you, H. I'm with you.

*Daz pulls Ray's jacket down over his shoulders and
ties the end of the sleeves together then punches him
again in the face, knocking him unconscious.*

H (*pulls out the gun*) Get away from him.

Daz Put that away, H.

H (*signals with the gun*) Get over there.

Daz (*to H*) Put it away.

H Move.

Daz (*to H*) I don't have a problem with you, H.

H Fuckin move.

Daz H, you gotta listen to me.

H Move over there.

Daz (*moves towards H*) Think of what he done to you, H. He fucked off an left you in the shit. (*Continues moving towards H.*) Come on, think about it. This is payback time.

H Why didn't you tell me who you were?

Daz I needed to see if I could trust you. I needed to see if you was bullshittin me. Settin me up. (*Beat.*) Now I know you weren't, it's fine.

H (*points the gun at Daz*) Get back.

    Daz stops.

I'll fuckin shoot you.

Daz Okay. (*Beat.*) But you should listen to me first.

    Pause.

I've got the gear, H.

    Pause.

I've got the gear here with me.

    Pause.

I'm gonna pick up my bag. (*He moves towards his bag.*)

H Don't do anythin.

Daz I'm gonna pick up my bag. (*He bends down and picks it up.*) I'm gonna show you, H. (*He puts the bag on the bed and unzips it.*) There's two kilos of charlie in here. (*He pulls out a large black-plastic-wrapped block of cocaine.*) Two kilos.

Pause.

Two keys of pure fuckin Peruvian product.

Pause.

We cut it into four. It's a hundred grand, H.

Pause.

We walk away.

Pause.

You've got the passport I need, H. (*Beat.*) I've got the gear you need.

Pause.

We walk away.

Pause.

We walk away.

Pause.

Yeah?

H nods.

Daz Good.

Pause.

Now shoot him.

H What?

Daz (*indicates Ray*) Shoot him.

Pause.

H Shoot him?

Daz Yeah. (*Beat.*) Fuckin shoot him.

Pause.

H I can't.

Daz Why can't you?

Pause.

H The noise . . .

Daz C'mon, fuckin shoot him. (*Beat.*) Shoot him in that big fuckin pumpkin head. In that big fuckin double-crossin scouse mouth.

Pause.

Yeah. (*Beat.*) I know Ray. (*Beat.*) I know he stitched you up.

Pause.

Two years, H. (*Beat.*) An him sitting there in his big fuck-off house.

Pause.

Two fuckin years.

Pause.

Now shoot him.

Long pause. Takes the gun from H's hand in one swift movement. Shakes his head. He opens the chamber of the gun in front of H's face.

You didn't even have one in the chamber. (*He shows H the empty chamber.*) See what happens when you have gaps in your education? (*Loads a round into the chamber of the gun.*) There's one in there now. (*Beat.*) No gaps in my education. (*Points the gun at H.*) Give me the passports.

H takes the passports from his pocket and gives them to Daz.

Daz Sit down.

H sits. Daz pulls a plastic cuff from his pocket.

D'you wanna drink? (*He ties the cuff round H's wrists.*) Go on, have a drink. (*Goes to the mini-bar.*) D'you want one?

H (*to Daz*) Listen, mate. Just take whatever you want.

Daz Yeah.

H Take it all.

Daz I will. (*Comes back with a bottle of beer. He opens it.*) Sorry about earlier an that. Playin dumb an everythin. Lyin.

Pause.

No hard feelins, yeah?

Daz feeds H the drink.

Daz (*indicates Ray*) And don't take it out on him. He didn't really grass. (*Puts the bottle of beer down on the table.*) This is a bit of a fuckin dilemma, innit?

Ray starts to come round.

Ray What the fuck . . .

Daz Funny things, dilemmas.

H Listen, mate. I've made a fuckin mistake here.

Daz You're fuckin right you've made a mistake. You've both made a fuckin mistake.

Ray tries to sit up.

H (*indicates Ray*) He's in some real shit back home.

Daz He's in the shit now.

H I got it wrong.

Daz It's too late.

H He's got a kid

Ray looks at H. Still dazed, he opens his mouth to speak but doesn't make any sound.

Daz It's funny. (*Beat.*) I wasn't supposed to be comin here today. There was another lad supposed to be doin it. (*Beat.*) See, they needed this bloke shot. An the lad that's goin to do it, the lad that was supposed to be comin over here, he's sittin there outside the bloke's house. Sniper rifle, scope, the fuckin lot. (*Beat.*) Anyway, the bloke comes out an the lad that's doin the job, he suddenly pulls up. Can't fuckin do it. He won't shoot him cos he's got a kiddie in his arms?

Pause.

He obviously had a dilemma.

Pause.

Me. (*Beat.*) I'd have shot him an the kiddie. Saves problems in the fuckin future, dunnit.

Ray (*looks at H*) What the fuck . . .

Daz You think you have a dilemma.

Ray (*looks at Daz*) What the fuck's goin on?

Daz (*punches Ray viciously in the face again*) But there's no dilemma. (*Beat.*) Never is, is there?

Pause.

You know who had a dilemma, H?

Pause.

C'mon, H. (*Beat.*) You're an educated man. (*Picks up the bag with the fake money and places it on the bed beside his own.*) Your Danish biker mate might know?

Pause.

I like books too, H. (*Beat.*) There's a lot of hangin around doin fuck-all in the forces, yeah. I guess it ain't so far away from doin all that time. (*Beat.*) *Hamlet*'s good innit? (*Beat.*) Really fuckin good. (*Beat.*) But it falls down for me on one thing. (*Beat.*) He's supposed to have a dilemma?

Pause.

Where's his fuckin dilemma? (*Beat.*) He doesn't do somethin, he's fucked. How much time does he think he's got moochin round the fuckin castle botherin skulls? (*Beat.*) His bird's mad. His mum's shaggin the bloke who slotted his dad an took over. This bloke's cheated him out of his fuckin birthright. Totally stitched him up. An if he's got any doubt about it, his old man's come back from beyond the grave an fuckin told him. (*Beat.*) He's fucked an he thinks he's got a fuckin dilemma. (*Beat.*) What's he got to lose? Nothin. (*Beat.*) What's he got to gain? Everythin. (*Beat.*) Slot the king an take over. Slot his mum. Throw his bird off the fuckin battlements an slot any fucker who moans. (*Beat.*) Where's his fuckin dilemma? (*Opens H's holdall and takes one of the blocks of money from it. He looks at the notes.*) Darwin. (*Beat.*) He was another one who got it wrong. (*He places the money in the bag. He picks up the passports.*) These passports are fuckin great, by the way. (*He puts them in the holdall.*) I can disappear now. No fuckin problem. (*Beat.*) Car. Bugle. Passports. Money. Gun. (*He laughs.*) An no dilemma.

H So who are you, mate?

Daz Who am I?

H Yeah.

Daz I just told you.

H Who d'you know?

Daz Who do I know?

H Yeah.

Pause.

Daz I know you.

Pause.

H I could do a job for you.

Daz I'm sure you could. (*He goes to the table and scrapes the remainder of the coke into a bag and puts it in his pocket.*)

H Think of the contacts I've got. The stuff we could do.

Daz I've retired.

H No you haven't.

Daz I have.

Pause. Ray begins to come round again.

Daz That's what I don't like about this business. That's why it ain't for me.

Pause.

You can run an run an run an run. Keep on movin. Keep hustlin. But you always have to come together some time. In a room. To do a deal.

Pause.

That's what fucks things up, innit? Other people. We all end up fucked in the end, because of other people. (*Picks up the holdall.*) You're alright, H.

H So let me go, then.

Daz Bein' alright ain't enough.

Pause.

You gotta be good.

Daz goes over to H. He picks up a piece of the tape that held the passports under the desk.

H One thing, mate?

Daz (*stops*) Yeah.

H How the fuck did you get them to put you in the same cell as me?

Daz (*smiles, puts the tape on H's mouth*) That was luck, mate.

Pause.

I've been lucky. (*Pats H on the head.*) Thank fuck I met you, H.

Daz leaves the room. Ray struggles against the jacket that ties him. H sits motionless.

Blackout.

The End.